CW00793780

RE-IMAGINING THE AVANT-GARDE

Revisiting the Architecture
of the 1960s and 1970s

GUEST-EDITED BY
MATTHEW BUTCHER AND
LUKE CASPAR PEARSON

ARCHITECTURAL DESIGN
July/August 2019
Profile No 260

Steel

NEMESTUDIO, Island of Steel,
Nine Islands: Matters Around Architecture,
2016

OMA,
Fondaco dei Tedeschi,
Venice,
2016

ISSN 0003-8504
ISBN 978 1119 506850

Guest-edited by **Matthew Butcher and Luke Caspar Pearson**

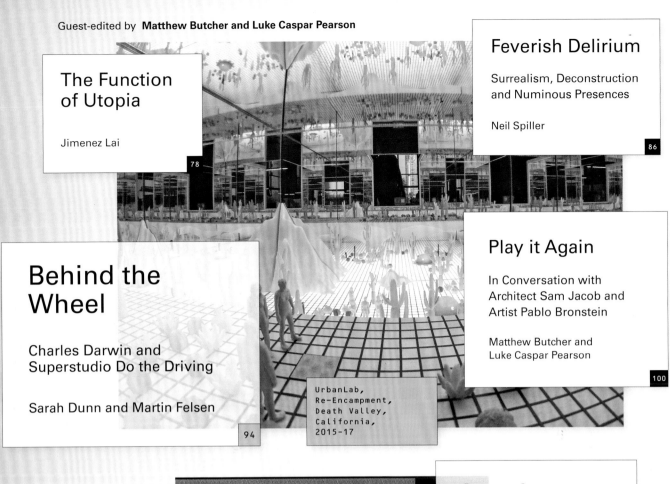

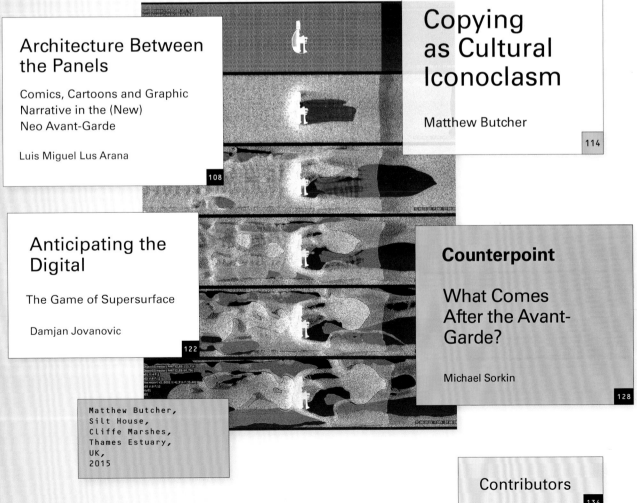

UrbanLab,
Re-Encampment,
Death Valley,
California,
2015-17

Matthew Butcher,
Silt House,
Cliffe Marshes,
Thames Estuary,
UK,
2015

Editorial Offices
John Wiley & Sons
9600 Garsington Road
Oxford
OX4 2DQ

T +44 (0)1865 776868

Editor
Neil Spiller

Commissioning Editor
Helen Castle

Managing Editor
Caroline Ellerby
Caroline Ellerby Publishing

Freelance Contributing Editor
Abigail Grater

Publisher
Paul Sayer

Art Direction + Design
CHK Design:
Christian Küsters
Barbara Nassisi

Production Editor
Elizabeth Gongde

Prepress
Artmedia, London

Printed in Italy by Printer
Trento Srl

Denise Bratton
Paul Brislin
Mark Burry
Helen Castle
André Chaszar
Nigel Coates
Peter Cook
Teddy Cruz
Max Fordham
Massimiliano Fuksas
Kate Goodwin
Edwin Heathcote
Anthony Hunt
Charles Jencks
Bob Maxwell
Brian McGrath
Jayne Merkel
Peter Murray
Kester Rattenbury
Mark Robbins
Deborah Saunt
Patrik Schumacher
Coren Sharples
Leon van Schaik
Claire Weisz
Ken Yeang
Alejandro Zaera-Polo

EDITORIAL BOARD

Journal Customer Services
For ordering information,
claims and any enquiry
concerning your journal
subscription please go to
www.wileycustomerhelp
.com/ask or contact your
nearest office.

Americas
E: cs-journals@wiley.com
T: +1 781 388 8598 or
+1 800 835 6770 (toll free
in the USA & Canada)

**Europe, Middle East
and Africa**
E: cs-journals@wiley.com
T: +44 (0)1865 778315

Asia Pacific
E: cs-journals@wiley.com
T: +65 6511 8000

Japan (for Japanese-
speaking support)
E: cs-japan@wiley.com
T: +65 6511 8010 or 005 316
50 480 (toll-free)

Visit our Online Customer
Help available in 7 languages
at www.wileycustomerhelp
.com/ask

Print ISSN: 0003-8504
Online ISSN: 1554-2769

Prices are for six issues
and include postage and
handling charges. Individual-
rate subscriptions must be
paid by personal cheque or
credit card. Individual-rate
subscriptions may not be
resold or used as library
copies.

All prices are subject to
change without notice.

Identification Statement
Periodicals Postage paid
at Rahway, NJ 07065.
Air freight and mailing in
the USA by Mercury Media
Processing, 1850 Elizabeth
Avenue, Suite C, Rahway,
NJ 07065, USA.

USA Postmaster
Please send address changes
to *Architectural Design*,
John Wiley & Sons Inc.,
c/o The Sheridan Press,
PO Box 465, Hanover,
PA 17331, USA

Rights and Permissions
Requests to the Publisher
should be addressed to:
Permissions Department
John Wiley & Sons Ltd
The Atrium
Southern Gate
Chichester
West Sussex PO19 8SQ
UK

F: +44 (0)1243 770 620
E: Permissions@wiley.com

All Rights Reserved. No
part of this publication
may be reproduced, stored
in a retrieval system or
transmitted in any form or
by any means, electronic,
mechanical, photocopying,
recording, scanning or
otherwise, except under
the terms of the Copyright,
Designs and Patents Act
1988 or under the terms
of a licence issued by the
Copyright Licensing Agency
Ltd, Barnard's Inn, 86 Fetter
Lane, London EC4A 1EN, UK,
without the permission in
writing of the Publisher.

Subscribe to Δ
Δ is published bimonthly
and is available to purchase
on both a subscription basis
and as individual volumes
at the following prices.

Prices
Individual copies:
£29.99 / US$45.00
Individual issues on
Δ App for iPad:
£9.99 / US$13.99
Mailing fees for print
may apply

Annual Subscription Rates
Student: £90 / US$137
print only
Personal: £136 / US$215
print and iPad access
Institutional: £310 / US$580
print or online
Institutional: £388 / US$725
combined print and online
6-issue subscription on
Δ App for iPad: £44.99 /
US$64.99

Front cover: Matthew
Butcher and Luke Caspar
Pearson, *Re-planning of
the Avant-Garde*, digital
collage, 2018. © Matthew
Butcher and Luke Caspar
Pearson

Inside front cover: Perry
Kulper, *Aerial Diptych
Folly, v.02: Oculus*, 2018.
© Perry Kulper

Page 1: NEMESTUDIO,
Plastic Pacific Hall, Middle
Earth: Dioramas for the
Planet, 2017. Courtesy of
NEMESTUDIO

04/2019

Δ | ARCHITECTURAL DESIGN

July/August
2019

Profile No.
260

Disclaimer
The Publisher and Editors cannot be held responsible
for errors or any consequences arising from the use
of information contained in this journal; the views and
opinions expressed do not necessarily reflect those of
the Publisher and Editors, neither does the publication
of advertisements constitute any endorsement by
the Publisher and Editors of the products advertised.

MIX
Paper from
responsible sources
FSC
www.fsc.org   FSC® C015829

Over the last decade, Matthew Butcher and Luke Pearson have been investigating the relevance of the architecture of the 1960s and 1970s within 21st-century architectural discourse, and ways of re-imagining this avant-garde work in contemporary design practices. This has underpinned both their research and teaching practice at the Bartlett School of Architecture, University College London (UCL), where Butcher is an Associate Professor of Architecture and Pearson a Lecturer in Architecture and Director of the Undergraduate Architecture Programme.

Butcher's research investigates how the innovative practices of the architectural avant-garde – incorporating art, land art and performance – might be re-enacted to address current environmental concerns. He explores how architects can develop a greater political, empathetic and physical relationship with the environments we inhabit, over one that is augmented by technology. His work has been exhibited at the Victoria and Albert Museum (V&A) in London; Storefront for Art and Architecture, New York; The Architecture Foundation, London; and the Prague Quadrennial. Recent projects and exhibitions include 2EmmaToc/Writtle Calling, a temporary radio station in Essex; Flood House, a floating architecture developed in collaboration with Jes Fernie and Focal Point Gallery in Southend; and Mansio, a retreat for writers and poets that visited sites along Hadrian's Wall in the summer of 2016. He is also the founder and Editor of the architectural newspaper *P.E.A.R.: Paper for Emerging Architectural Research*, and has contributed articles and papers for journals including *Architecture Research Quarterly* (*ARQ*), the *RIBA Journal* and *Architecture Today*. He currently holds a visiting lectureship at Umeå School of Architecture, Sweden, and a visiting professorship at Genoa Technical University in Italy.

Pearson's work explores the relationship between pop culture, technology and architectural design with reference to avant-garde projects of the past. He uses video-game technologies as new forms of architectural representation and generators of utopic environments, often adopting the analytical approaches of historical figures such as Robert Venturi and Denise Scott Brown to explore the formal composition of game spaces, for example in his doctoral research project Learning from Los Santos. He is co-founder (with Sandra Youkhana) of the design practice You+Pea, which works at the intersection of architecture, video games and experimental drawing. Recent commissions include Projectives, a video game based on Hans Vredeman de Vries's perspectival studies; the *Architecture (After Games)* installation at the V&A; and Peep-Pop City, an Archizoom-inspired game responding to London's urban morphology that was exhibited at Somerset House. He has lectured widely on this research, at the Strelka Institute, New York University Games Lab, the V&A and Asakusa Gallery Tokyo among others, and has been published in journals including the *Journal of Architectural Education*, *Thresholds* and *ARQ* alongside architecture and game-industry publications such as *CLOG: Sci-Fi*, *Architects' Sketchbooks*, *Heterotopias* and *EDGE* magazine. He is also the co-founder of 'Drawing Futures', an international conference and book series on drawing practices for art and architecture.

As guest-editors of this issue, Butcher and Pearson have worked together to frame the avant-garde not simply as a subject for historical enquiry, but as a catalyst for new forms of architectural practice and research. This has developed from their shared belief that work from this point in time, when the conceptual project of architectural modernity was being twisted and subverted, continues to resonate ever more strongly in the face of emerging technologies. ⊿

Text © 2019 John Wiley & Sons Ltd. Images: Photos by Sophie Percival

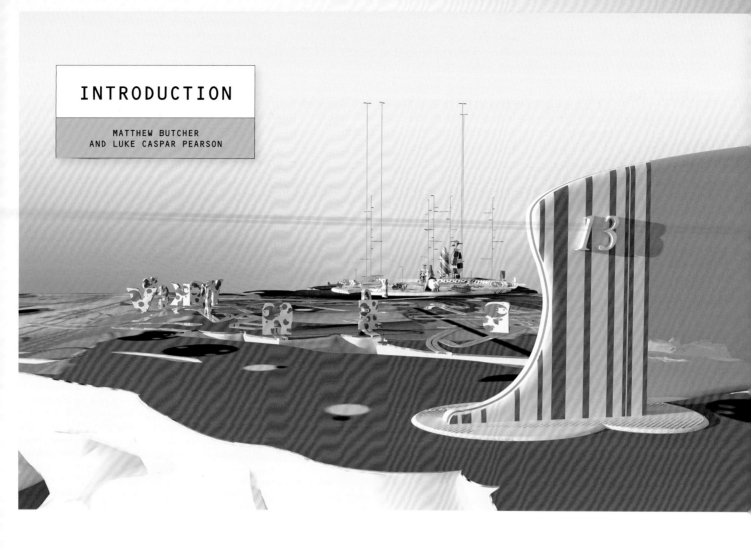

ENDURING EXPERIMENTS

How the Architectural Avant-Garde Lives On

The 1960s and 1970s saw a significant increase in architectural projects seeking to redefine the discipline, many of which have gone on to become seminal works. Loosely grouped together under the term 'avant-garde', these projects and ideologies remain highly influential today. Like the historical avant-garde of the early part of the 20th century, this 'neo' or 'late' avant-garde[1] was not singular in its formal, conceptual or political ambitions. It encompassed divergent geographic and cultural situations, with a wide variety of aims, representational techniques and political views – differences that existed even among the protagonists of individual subsections such as the Italian Radical movement emerging from Florence or the Whites and Grays stationed on the East Coast of the US. Their common objective, however, was to assert architecture once again as an autonomous discipline, as a political provocateur and a means of social satire.

The conceptual and often contradictory nature of the projects lends them a timeless presence; as Pino Brugellis and Manuel Orazi argue of the Italian Radicals, 'they are susceptible to different interpretations and meanings, without ever exhausting their explosive charge: a sort of architectural Big Bang that continues to expand today, while keeping alive the chaos of its origins'.[2] The period produced reflections on issues such as the looming ecological crisis, the Vietnam War, Modernism's increasing focus on market-driven ideals of efficiency and technology, and a shift in society to a condition of hyper-consumerism.[3] For historian Marco De Michelis, this neo-avant-garde was an eclectic group of 'architects, philosophers, and historians, whose diverse ideas were connected only by a common determination to alter the obsolete tenets of modernist practice and to reevaluate architecture in terms of the new imperatives of the postwar world'.[4]

This issue of _D_ seeks to explore this ambition and energy in the context of contemporary architectural practice. It examines the work of the 1960s and 1970s as a historical precedent, a barometer of an experimental design ethos, framing its protagonists as instigators of new formal techniques. In doing so it illuminates the creativity inherent in methodologies that build reciprocity between this period and contemporary design cultures.

There have been many studies on the methods and motives of these historical projects. The intention of this issue is not to create a new history in the typical sense, but rather to represent how the influence of the historical avant-garde directly resonates with architectural practice some 50 years later. To understand its impact, the contributions are presented under four main themes: 'The Avant-Garde as Precedent', 'The Spirit of the Avant-Garde', 'Utopia' and 'Formal Repetition'.

Dogma with OFFICE Kersten Geers
David Van Severen,
City-Walls project for the New
Multifunctional Administrative City,
South Korea,
2005

Dogma, founded by Pier Vittorio Aureli and Martino Tattara, and OFFICE Kersten Geers David Van Severen, are recognised as key protagonists of the renewed interest in avant-garde architects working in the 1960s and 1970s. The proposed project, reminiscent of Archizoom's _No-Stop City_ (1969–1970), presents a city of external and habitable urban rooms formed from a superstructure of walls.

Perry Kulper,
El Dorado: Floating Bird Motel,
2017

Kulper's speculative project (see also pp 68–9) establishes a familiar strangeness through the juxtaposition of distant realities in a metaphorical resort proposal for birds, employing tactical manipulations of the absurd and fantastical, rendered as richly graphic worlds. Drawing in collaboration with Saumon Oboudiyat.

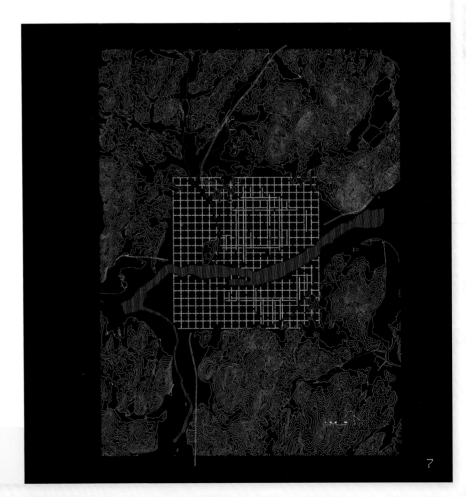

The Avant-Garde as Precedent

Today, references to Superstudio, Peter Eisenman, Archizoom and John Hejduk abound. By examining the reinterpretation and application of such avant-garde positions in current practices, the aim is to elucidate shared links between contemporary architects and those who serve as a historical vanguard. Given technological developments beyond anything the avant-gardes could have predicted, which have totally reshaped everything from the production of drawings to buildings and the notion of communication itself, why do architects continue to align their work with such a specific historical period and set of languages?

To start to investigate this idea, William Menking's article 'Superstudio as Super-Office' (pp 14–21) sheds light on the group's attempt to create a radical departure from the traditional architectural office. This was not only manifest in their drawn and theoretical work, but also in a desire to build buildings, which Menking sees as a means to subvert the discipline from within – a form of operation that resonates strongly with the work of contemporary practices such as raumlabor and Assemble.

Superstudio,
Saluti da Coketown,
1969

The work of radical architecture practice Superstudio and their ubiquitous gridded designs, ranging from tables and chairs to endless monuments, has become iconic of avant-garde work produced during the period. Their gridded world was a foreshadowing of our digital age, and their desire for architecture to act as artistic provocation towards the ongoing mobilisation of capital resonates just as strongly today.

raumlaborberlin,
Poster for the opening of Floating University,
Berlin,
2018

Presented as an anti-utopia, raumlaborberlin's work, while influenced by radical architects such as Superstudio, moves away from grand speculative statements to focus on the physical, environmental and political conditions of where the projects are sited. The Floating University, for example, was designed as a space for discourse on the future of urban living in Berlin.

In turn, Sarah Deyong (pp 22–9) emphasises how contemporary practice has drawn heavily from the avant-garde to develop an almost evangelical and 'hardcore' obsession with form. Expanding Postmodernism's desire to detach form from function, she argues that current trends see form as fluid, allowing for multiple interpretations and manipulations divorced from concerns about context, site and process.

When looking at contemporary practices' attempts at embodying the spirit of the avant-garde, it is important to register the influence of educational institutions, and none more so than the Architectural Association (AA) in London. During the 1970s and 1980s, the AA, headed by the enlightened Alvin Boyarsky, produced a new generation of experimental architects including Rem Koolhaas, Zaha Hadid and Nigel Coates. In his article 'Avant-Garde in the Age of Identity' (pp 30–37), Igor Marjanović looks at the very particular culture and innovation present in the school at this time, addressing how the notions of identity being expressed there informed its design output and are still helping to define educational practice today.

Encapsulating both the stylistic and theoretical framework of this neo avant-garde is San Francisco-based NEMESTUDIO. In his interview with partner Neyran Turan (pp 38–45), architect and historian Stylianos Giamarelos reveals the importance of this period in the studio's work, and how it has helped them to establish critical methodologies to address geographical and environmental issues in their own research and to explore new forms of architectural practice.

As a counterpoint to the celebration of, and reference to, groups such as Superstudio, architectural writer and commentator Mimi Zeiger warns of the dangers of historic reverence and reinvention without a critical purpose (pp 46–53). Architecture must be wary of retreating to an endless 'Groundhog Day' of historical loops that the discipline might currently be accused of engaging with. Instead, she argues, architecture must challenge its references from within, and against other forms of practice and distinct political and social contexts.

The Spirit of the Avant-Garde

The spirit of the neo avant-gardes, like their forebears the Surrealists and Dadaists, was driven by a desire to develop polemics through and against existing cultural hegemonies, in their case the discipline of architecture. Their work took many forms, manifesting as drawings and texts, luscious graphic illustrations, self-published magazines, performances and small-scale installations and structures. The Information Age, however, has done much to change both how and in what context architectural imagery is now created and disseminated.

Andrew Kovacs (pp 54–61) explains how his constantly updated Archive of Affinities project, a collection of scanned and recorded images shared online, explores the meaning and purpose of contemporary relationships with historical architectural imagery within the context of social media platforms and the Internet, and how the construction of this digital archive has informed his development of new propositions and ways of working as a designer.

Perry Kulper's work exudes the spirit of the speculative, the critical and the wonderful through an expansive set of detailed drawings and collages. In his contribution to this issue (pp 62–9) he sets out to trace the historical and neo avant-garde influences behind his work, and discusses how the adoption of digital tools has allowed him to work free from concerns for such fundamentals as time and gravity.

Ant Farm,
Dolphin Embassy,
1974

A key avant-garde reference point for several of the contributors to this issue of *D* is the seminal group Ant Farm. Producing work across installations, performance and media events, they stretched the parameters of what was considered architecture in the late 1960s and 1970s. The drawing shows a floating boat-like structure that was designed to foster greater communication and interaction between dolphins and humans.

Surveying the avant-garde's fascination with technology, Luke Pearson (pp 70–77) demonstrates a correlation between the negative utopias of avant-garde radicals such as Archizoom, and the spatial, temporal and formal possibilities of contemporary computer games and their manifestations of virtual space. For him, this link to Archizoom's conception of the city as an isotropic grid could open up new worlds that bridge the gap between the actual and the theoretical, logic and representation, philosophies he investigates with reference to several of his game-based architectural environments.

Utopia

The creation of utopias was fundamental to many of the most seminal projects of the period, mirroring society and underpinning architectural critiques. Utopia persists in architecture today, and as Jimenez Lai suggests (pp 78–85), is a mechanism for architects to operate as 'journalists', using the design of spaces to communicate and narrate the world back to us through new lenses. Lai's own drawing directly tackles the representational structures architects use, and as such the ways in which architecture continues to frame Utopia.

Luke Pearson demonstrates a correlation between the negative utopias of avant-garde radicals such as Archizoom, and the spatial, temporal and formal possibilities of contemporary computer games and their manifestations of virtual space

Luke Caspar Pearson,
Inflection,
2015

Drawing from architecture theory and precedent, Pearson's work explores virtual game worlds as new vehicles for utopic architecture. In *Inflection*, inspired by Robert Venturi's definition of fragmentary ordering logics in architectural form, player interactions cause inflected elements to grow and reveal their true formal continuity over time in a virtual architecture.

Archizoom,
No-Stop City,
1969–70

Archizoom co-opted and critiqued the spaces of the hyper-capitalist reality they saw emerging with imperialist precision in the 1960s, a condition that is even more pervasive today. Utilising the infinite gridded spaces and organisational forms of the supermarket and office building, they proposed an endless architecture that would free us from the burdens of work into a realm of endless play.

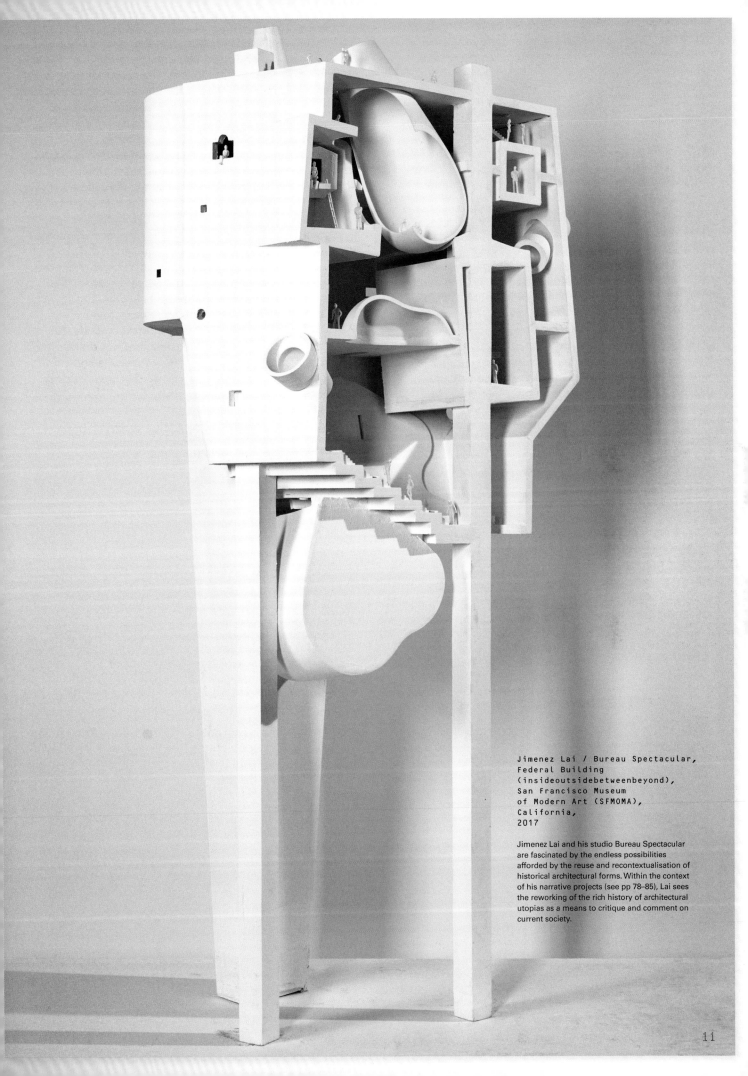

Jimenez Lai / Bureau Spectacular,
Federal Building
(insideoutsidebetweenbeyond),
San Francisco Museum
of Modern Art (SFMOMA),
California,
2017

Jimenez Lai and his studio Bureau Spectacular
are fascinated by the endless possibilities
afforded by the reuse and recontextualisation of
historical architectural forms. Within the context
of his narrative projects (see pp 78–85), Lai sees
the reworking of the rich history of architectural
utopias as a means to critique and comment on
current society.

The utopian can also be seen not simply as a vision of the future, but as an organising structure that binds the logic of a world together. As Neil Spiller argues (pp 86–93), his work is not 'utopian' in the conventional sense (or perhaps in any sense). Yet within his 20-year Communicating Vessels project, which circumvents myths, impossible spaces and the looming presence of new technologies, we find links once again to those 'negative utopias' of the avant-garde in worlds where the protocols of architectural representation, technology and fantasy could be energised as a political vehicle.

Utopias and negative utopias of the avant-garde were also notable for addressing the environmental context of the day. In fact, as Sarah Dunn and Martin Felsen of UrbanLab show us (pp 94–9), the relationship between utopia and ecological systems is a long one. From Charles Darwin to Kenzo Tange and their own proposals for Lake Michigan, the cultivation of landscape is a recurring theme in utopic architecture. This is made even more relevant when such endeavours involve the creation of utopias as systems allowing for change rather than fixed proposals, reflecting its importance as a design mechanism, and one that keenly corresponds to developments in computational technologies.

Formal Repetition

One of the key implications of looking back at the avant-garde is to understand the significance of formal tropes at risk of losing their agency due to the fluidity of modern imagery. In a lively conversation with the Guest-Editors of this issue (pp 100–107), architect Sam Jacob and artist Pablo Bronstein show the acts of repetition and re-enactment as important ways of using architectural history in contemporary design practice. This could be the adoption of a particular character or working method, but also assuming a mindset, an ethic for approaching architecture and form.

Avant-garde architects of the 1960s and 1970s challenged the discipline by expanding the media field through which architecture could be approached to clothing, furniture, inflatables and comic books. In a comic specially commissioned for this issue (pp 108–11), Luis Miguel Lus Arana and architectural cartoonist Klaus take us on a journey through this expanded field, tracing paths from the neo avant-gardes to contemporary practitioners who continue to push at the edges of what we might consider to be architecture. Klaus's architectural caricatures reassemble the iconography of the avant-garde into a new formal history.

Given their iconic status, Matthew Butcher (pp 114–22) suggests we should develop more nuanced positions towards these historical avant-garde projects, eschewing blank reverence. His article examines his own design practice in relation to the works of Superstudio and Raimund Abraham, where the agency of both iconophilia and iconoclasm, the love and destruction of images can be developed into a holistic design practice. In his case, this relationship between form and history is carried through into the design of specific structures where distortions of avant-garde drawings become encoded into material forms. This iconoclasm is productive,

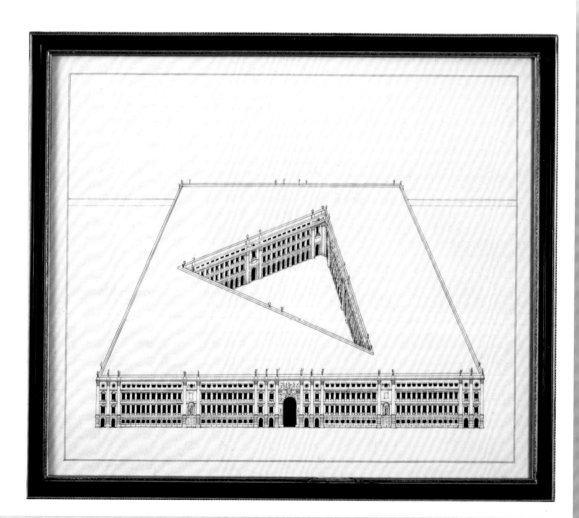

Pablo Bronstein,
Large Building with Courtyard,
2005

Over the last 15 years, Bronstein's work has been developed through methods of role play, a device employed to allow the artist to embody historical architectural styles and characterisations in his illusory architectural projections. His work (see also pp 100–107) references avant-garde design of the 1960s and 1970s as well as the 18th century, creating complex collages of history and time.

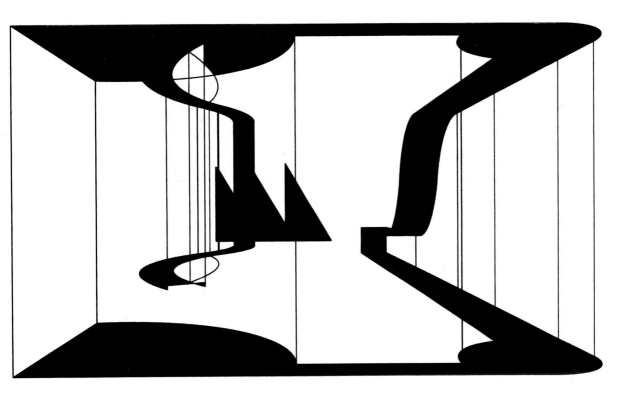

Matthew Butcher,
Movement Notation 004,
2008

Inspired by methodologies of performance practice associated with notions of re-enactment, Butcher's work seeks to reinvigorate questions around what might constitute a contemporary avant-garde. In his *Notations* series, he worked with a choreographer to create complex movement notations that were inspired by Bernard Tschumi's seminal *Manhattan Transcripts* (1976–81) project.

generating an ongoing memorialisation rather than a frozen and fixed history.

In many ways the work of avant-garde groups like Superstudio and Archizoom predicted the digital worlds we inhabit today. As Damjan Jovanovic points out (pp 122–5), Superstudio's expansive grid is now not only a visual feedback loop (as mentioned by Mimi Zeiger), but is also the organising principle of our digital world. His discussion of his Supersurface computer-game application as an extension of architectural media recalls William Menking's exploration of how the avant-garde imagination and working methods rupture the boundaries of the discipline.

Continuing Contradictions

In re-imagining the avant-garde of the 1960s and 1970s, this Δ issue brings together contributors who establish resonance between this period and the cutting-edge design experiments we are seeing today. This historical moment continues to fascinate because, as Brugellis and Orazi continue, 'the strength of those works lies precisely in their unabashed staging of the contradictions of those years, which are unfortunately the conflicts and contradictions of the present time and perhaps of the near future.'[5]

The consumerist society in which the avant-garde emerged – and in many cases directly critiqued – has expanded; the ecological crisis is reaching a zenith and social unrest has grown with the rise in populist politics.

Within this context it is both relevant and pressing to readdress questions of how architecture can once more align itself with a period that established, in the words of K Michael Hays, 'a moment in history when certain ways of practicing architecture still had philosophical aspirations'.[6] *Re-imagining the Avant-Garde* roots out the architects of today who hold on to this philosophical underpinning, whose work bounces back and forth between reference and reinvention, building the case that such practices define a significant moment in contemporary architectural discourse in which we can seek to cross temporal boundaries. Δ

Notes
1. The term 'neo avant-garde' as described by Peter Burger refers to cultural production that utilised forms from the historical avant-garde. The term 'late avant-garde' was developed by K Michael Hays in order to separate his understanding of this period of architectural production from others. See Peter Burger, *Theory of the Avant-Garde*, trans Michael Shaw, University of Minnesota Press (Minneapolis, MN), 1984, p 148, and K Michael Hays, *Architecture's Desire: Reading the Late Avant-Garde*, MIT Press (Cambridge, MA), 2010, pp 4–12.
2. Pino Brugellis and Manuel Orazi, 'Radicals Forever', in Pino Brugellis, Gianni Pettena and Alberto Salvadori (eds), *Radical Utopias*, Quodlibet Habitat (Rome), 2017, p 38.
3. Hilde Heynen, *Architecture and Modernity*, MIT Press (Cambridge, MA), 1999, pp 4–5, 149–53.
4. Marco De Michelis, 'Aldo Rossi and Autonomous Architecture', in Terence Riley *et al* (eds), *The Changing of the Avant-Garde: Visionary Architectural Drawing from the Howard Gilman Collection*, Museum of Modern Art (New York), 2002, p 90.
5. Brugellis and Orazi, *op cit.*
6. Hays, *op cit*, p 1.

Text © 2019 John Wiley & Sons Ltd. Images: p 6 © Perry Kulper; p 7 Dogma in collaboration with OFFICE Kersten Geers David Van Severen; p 8(t) © raumlaborberlin / Victoria Tomaschko; p 8(b) MAXXI National Museum of the XXI Century Arts, Rome MAXXI Architecture Collection; p 9 Drawing by Curtis Schreier. Image courtesy of the University of California, Berkeley Art Museum and Pacific Film Archive; p 10(t) © Luke Caspar Pearson; p 10(b) © Studio Andrea Branzi; p 11 © Jimenez Lai; p 12 Courtesy the artist and Herald St, London; p 13 © Matthew Butcher

SUPER AS SUPER

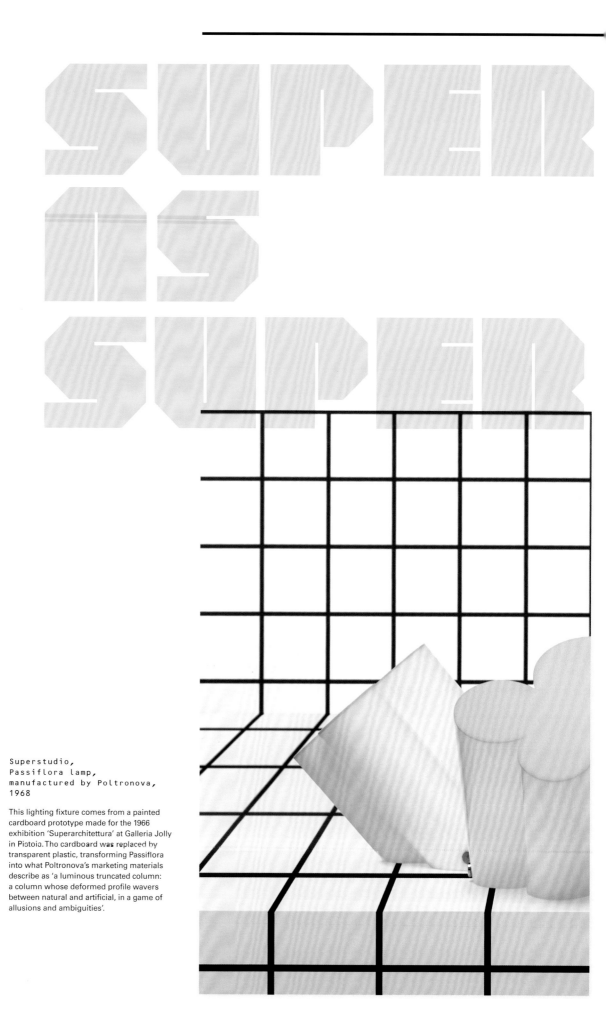

Superstudio,
Passiflora lamp,
manufactured by Poltronova,
1968

This lighting fixture comes from a painted
cardboard prototype made for the 1966
exhibition 'Superarchitettura' at Galleria Jolly
in Pistoia. The cardboard was replaced by
transparent plastic, transforming Passiflora
into what Poltronova's marketing materials
describe as 'a luminous truncated column:
a column whose deformed profile wavers
between natural and artificial, in a game of
allusions and ambiguities'.

STUDIO

William Menking

OFFICE

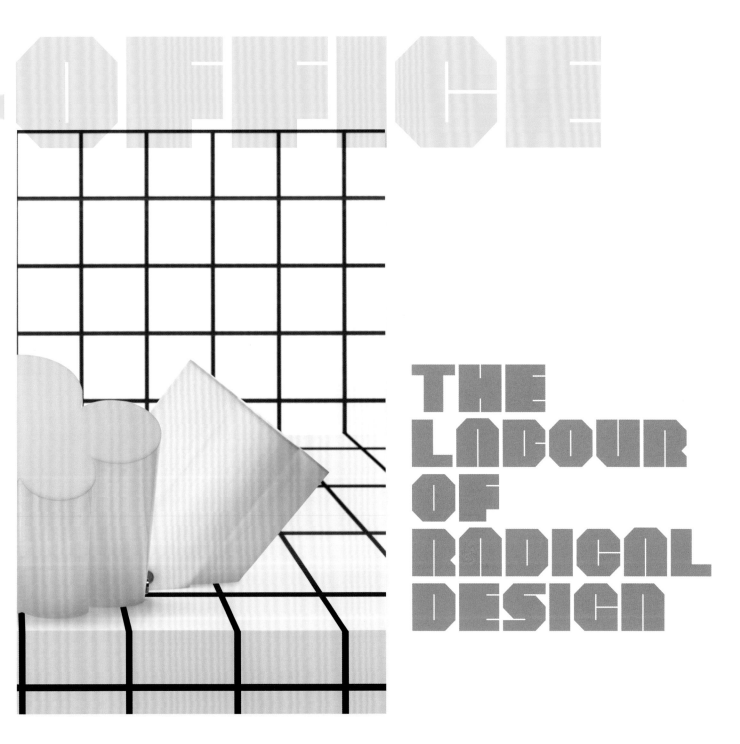

THE LABOUR OF RADICAL DESIGN

Key avant-garde players are often assumed to be divorced from the reality of practice. In the case of Superstudio, this assumption is wildly inaccurate. **William Menking**, co-founder and Editor-in-Chief of *The Architect's Newspaper* and Professor at Pratt Institute, New York, co-organised the 2003 exhibition 'Superstudio: Life Without Objects' with Peter Lang. Here he puts right some myths about the nature of this well-known but much-misunderstood Florentine collaborative, setting it in the context of the intellectual and industrial climate of 1960s Italy, and exploring how its approach can inspire those seeking to rethink practice today.

The architect's suicide and the disappearance of architecture are two equivalent phenomena: to work towards the one or the other is only a question of quantity. In both cases, it means eliminating the formal structures connected to the artificial scale of values.

In this sense, our work has used the instruments of architecture in a contrary fashion, gradually, through absurdity, showing its uselessness, its falsity and its immorality.

—Adolfo Natalini, Architectural Association School of Architecture lecture,
London, 3 March 1971[1]

It is now over 10 years since 'Parametricism' was declared 'the great new style after modernism'.[2] But while the role of computation in experimental material research and design is undeniable, the application of the computer to the design and production of buildings has also facilitated an increased regimentation and corporatisation of design practice and architectural production. In day-to-day practice the working environment in the typical architect's office has increasingly become one of disconnection, repetition of labour, lack of cooperation and, in the long term, dehumanisation and a loss of cognitive skills. The issues of architectural labour in a globalised economy are among the most important for young practitioners and are the derivation of research and advocacy groups like the American groups The Architecture Lobby and Who Builds Your Architecture?.[3]

Many firms are trying to rethink how their highly organised command and control structures might be rearranged to better handle the massive information flows now available through distributed computing, autonomous modelling systems and artificial intelligence coming into their offices. But these firms are usually reinforcing their existing structure, rather than thinking more creatively how best to create a better, more equal shared working culture. This shift from a traditional architectural command-and-control structure to a less corporate model requires a total cultural change, and most firms are not able or are unwilling to make this leap in how work is carried out in daily practice.

New Models of Architectural Labour
Many young architects are pushing back against this corporate structure and creating new, less hierarchical modes of practice. Perhaps because they are newly formed, more

Cover of *D*,
no 12,
1971

The cover photo shows Superstudio in their office at 1 via di Bellosguardo, Florence. From left to right: Cristiano Toraldo di Francia, Alessandro Magris, Roberto Magris, Adolfo Natalini, Gianpiero Frassinelli and Alessandro Poli. On the table is their purple *Hidden Architecture*, published in *Design Quarterly* in January 1971.

Warehouse of Architecture
and Research (WAR),
Il Dramun,
2018

Il Dramun, or 'drama by moonlight', is WAR's
attempt to creatively represent one of its housing
projects – currently ongoing near the cities of
Pesaro and Urbino – in comic-book story form
to reflect its architectural design in a way that
captures attention, evocative of the soap opera's
simple storytelling. Although digitally produced,
it is clearly influenced by the storyboard-form
drawings of Superstudio as presented, for
example, in their *Fundamental Acts* (1971–3).

attuned to the possibilities of a shared working environment,
working outside the market or simply desiring a more
equal decision-making process, many are creating new
forms of professional practice. These studios realise that the
possibilities of shared practice are actually enhanced because
of the computer.

New approaches to architectural labour can be seen in
various forms in the work of two international groupings of
like-minded designers. One group might include Sam Jacob
in London, Olalekan Jeyifous in Brooklyn, and Warehouse
of Architecture and Research (WAR) in Rome. This is the
'digitally averse' group that Mario Carpo derisively calls
'the Post-digitalists' or the PoDigs, though these practices
and individuals have more refined and radical notions of
computation and culture than Carpo would allow.[4]
A second group proposing new models of work are
collaboratives like raumlabor (in Berlin), Assemble (in
London), Crimson (in Rotterdam), FACE Design (in New
York) and Traumnovelle (in Brussels). These groups are
fluid and multidisciplinary in nature, often made up of not
only architects, but informal groupings of social scientists,
artists and craftspeople. They are frequently professionals
inexperienced in design studio culture, formed and hardened
in architecture schools, and they expect a decision-making
process that works horizontally across production and
research decisions, not top-down or hierarchical. The groups
all claim to champion interdisciplinary, often open-system
practice with architecture at the centre of their projects.

raumlabor,
Floating University,
Berlin,
2018

A summer learning centre in a rainwater basin, designed as a
place where transdisciplinary research teams consider the complex
questions of urban practice like how cities might cope with risks,
strains and chances of global warming, resource shortages, super-
diversity and hyper-accelerated development.

Traumnovelle,
Ode to Joy,
2018

Traumnovelle describe themselves
as a 'militant faction' of three
Belgian architects. They, like
Superstudio, claim to follow a
multidisciplinary approach with
'architecture at the crossroads'
and acknowledge their landscape
collage technique.

History of Non-Traditional Practice

This idea of a group architectural practice, where individuals bring different skills and abilities into a collaborative design process, goes back to at least the 1960s and groups like Archigram (in London), Ant Farm (in San Francisco), Utopie (in Paris) and others. These media-savvy groups remain role models for their powerful utopian image making, but also for their multidisciplinary approach and working structure. Today's younger practices and figures seeking new ways of work all look back, often romantically, to the period of the 1960s and 1970s for inspiration, and to the Italian 'design Radicals' – particularly Superstudio, founded in Florence in 1966 by Adolfo Natalini and Cristiano Toraldo di Francia.[5]

Jacopo Costanzo, from the Roman group WAR, claims a generational affinity with Superstudio and says 'we learned from them to question the system, to take care with storytelling and how to represent projects'.[6] But he also believes the 'heterogeneity of the Florentines' working studio method' is a crucial part of their legacy for current generations.[7] 'They were,' he says *'complex and contradictory* as a team, with deep differences, but every project they made was strong, clear and synthetic'.[8]

Beyond the images they produced, what makes Superstudio's working method and practice relevant to today's practitioners? It is important first to put right a widespread misconception about how the Italian group practised from their founding until 1973, when they entered into the larger collaborative design group Global Tools and began to break apart as a functioning collective. Benjamin Foerster-Baldenius, from raumlabor, admires Superstudio and says 'yes 70s utopian groups have influenced us – it's obvious, no? The difference is that we work out there in reality.'[9] This idea that Superstudio did not work 'out there in reality' and focused only on theoretical propositions and later art installations is a common misunderstanding about the Florentines, fed by statements of theirs like the one calling 'for the architect's public suicide' or when they declared 'design must disappear, we can live without architecture'.[10]

Superstudio,
Competition design for
a school in La Spezia,
Italy,
1968

Superstudio as a professional
office entered competitions and
hoped to win and build their
designs. This drawing and collage
illustrates their *Continuous
Monument* grid and their
'theory-practice-theory check'
way of working.

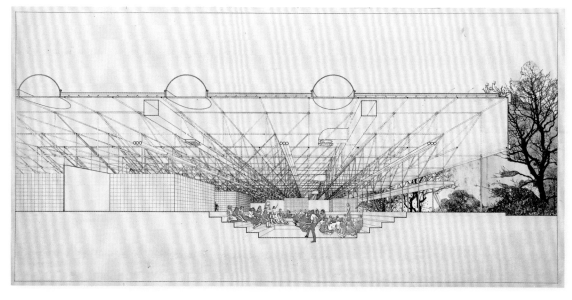

Superstudio,
Collage of the Superstudio office
at 1 via di Bellosguardo,
Florence,
1973

Created for an exhibition at the Neue Galerie Graz, Austria,
this is a theoretical not actual depiction of Superstudio's
working office. Despite their reputation as theorists, they
are pictured here as practising architects.

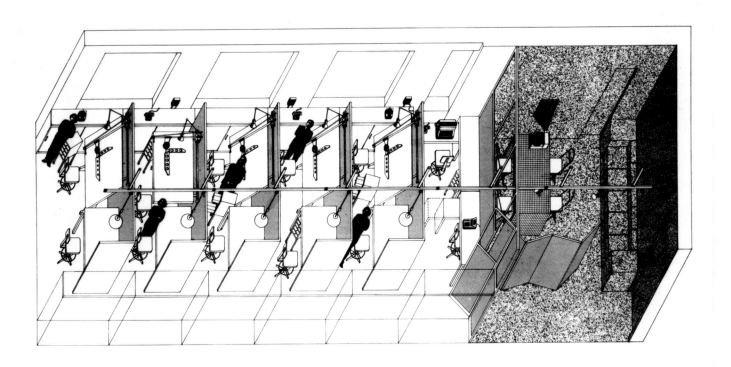

Superstudio,
Design for a hotel in the Coliseum,
Rome,
1969

Superstudio's building project is clearly unbuildable
because of its location in the Roman Coliseum but a
concept that is entirely realisable.

Labour Inside Superstudio

During the preparation of the catalogue for the exhibition
'Superstudio: Life Without Objects', which was first shown
at London's Design Museum in 2003, multiple conversations
with members of the group – particularly Gianpiero
Frassinelli and Adolfo Natalini[11] – revealed that while their
work has used the instruments of architecture in a contrary
fashion, as a working group they intended to transform
architecture from inside the profession and wanted to
practise 'architecture'.[12]

They were not proposing that architects give up on the
profession, as their contemporary critic Manfredo Tafuri
argued, or become artists or anthropologists.[13] It is easy to
read their 1973 *Project Zeno* as a call for designers to focus
on planning or anthropology, or the 1978 installation *The
Wife of Lot* as architects working as artists at the Venice art
biennale. Peter Lang points out how Superstudio differed
from the other Florentine Radicals:

> Superstudio embarked on a 'classical' architectural
> trajectory, effectively campaigning to destabilize modern
> architecture while remaining within the enlightenment
> language of perspectival space … they did not …
> seek to challenge the conventions of representation,
> or the projection of two-dimensional singular ocular
> perspective, but to subvert the principles of architecture
> within this convention.[14]

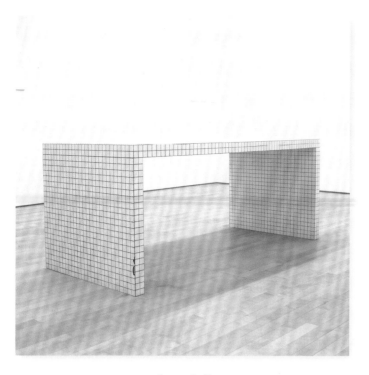

Superstudio,
Table, manufactured by Zanotta,
1973

The table was presented at the Neue Galerie Graz, Austria and then went into commercially successful production – an illustration of Superstudio's 'theory-practice-theory check' which stemmed from a combination of the particular conditions of craft production and the overheated intellectual atmosphere in Italy at the time.

In fact, Superstudio's ubiquitous black-on-white grids, used so powerfully in their *Continuous Monument* series (1969), might be understood as refined architectural language used to poetically communicate their thinking with other designers. Given the experiments in perspective by architects and artists in Renaissance Florence, the use of the grid had a special resonance for the members of the group. The 1971–3 Superstudio series *Fundamental Acts* (*Life, Education, Ceremony, Love, Death*), they claim in *Casabella* magazine, is a plea specifically to architects 'to engage or re-engage in the profession', and they emphasised the 'fundamental themes of our life'.[15] Further they conclude the Acts by stating 'the attempt to regenerate architecture both anthropologically and philosophically becomes the core of our reductive process'.[16] Even their collaboration in the 1973 super-group Global Tools can be understood as a last attempt to reform, not leave, the profession.

In order to understand Superstudio's formation as a collective it is important to be aware that it came together at the time of Italy's 'economic miracle'.[17] This was the time of the creation of a consumer and rebellious youth culture in the country and the specific conditions of Italian 'collective action'.[18] But to understand Superstudio's 'classical trajectory', it is more important to go back to their founding at the University of Florence and the special architectural culture of the Tuscan city.

Italian Architectural Education in the 1960s

Italian architectural education in the 1960s was unique and, with no centralised education or professional standards in place, each school, as Peter Lang argues, had its 'own archaic system' that 'effectively managed to create a sort of permanent antagonistic relationship between a cast of characters that included the administrations, the faculty the students and that carried on throughout most of the 1960s'.[19] Located in major urban centres – Rome, Milan, Venice and Florence – each was dominated by local architects and intellectual figures. In Rome, Bruno Zevi created a school inspired by the organicism of American architect Frank Lloyd Wright (1867–1959); Milan focused on industrial production; and Venice was under the influence of the historical and theoretical writings of Manfredo Tafuri. Florence, dominated by a conservative local profession and ancient faculty, had its own dynamic that included the student occupation of administrators' offices (including by several of the Superstudio members) and the creation of a council of students and faculty. What made Florence unique was that the council's suggestions were taken up by faculty members like Leonardo Ricci and Leonardo Savioli, and this introduced an entirely new sensibility to the university's classes.[20] As Peter Lang writes, it kept education 'less concerned with an ideologically driven socially conditioned architecture … and far more interested in investigating new cultural phenomena and their impact on establishing new building technologies'.[21]

In particular, Ricci's hands-on experimental workshops promoted a multi-dimensional approach, including broad freedoms in composition strategies, materials, sculpture, film and music. Cristiano Toraldo di Francia claims this approach shook up the school and because the students were encouraged to take education into their own hands Superstudio formed as a collaborative focusing on theoretical media experiments, proposals and installations.[22] 'Radical Architecture,' Frassinelli claimed, 'was born in the occupied university'.[23]

In addition, Florence was home to a lively cultural, publishing and art scene. Maria Gloria Bicocchi's avant-garde gallery Centrodiffusionegrafica brought international artists to Florence including those featured in the New York-based magazine *Avalanche*, such as the Americans Dennis Oppenheim, Allan Kaprow, Vito Acconci and Bill Viola. Their presence served as inspiration for the Superstudio architects to remain professionals while addressing important contemporary social issues. Bicocchi (whose gallery assistant was the partner of Frassinelli) says about this period in Florence:

I think that everyone in Florence in those days (1971/74) was connected and influenced each other, centrodiffusionegrafica without Schema Zona, Superstudio, UFO, Archizoom and all the atmosphere of experimental culture would probably have not existed one without the other … we shared artists, exhibitions and ideas. We were very much tuned together![24]

Theory-Practice-Theory Check

Further, in the period when Superstudio produced their most important theoretical and artistic work they were simultaneously designing and building nightclubs, banks, private houses, furniture, lamps and even railway carriages. In this particularly Italian condition, as Lang notes, 'the process developed into a series of checks and balances whereby the theory engendered the production, and [was] subsequently re-theorised, controlled and modified'.[25] Superstudio's black-on-white *Continuous Monument* grid, for example, became a commercially successful line of tables, lamps and luxury household objects. Natalini claims Italian architects focused on designing luxury goods because so many were unemployed. In the Florence School of Architecture, he goes on, there were '6,000 students, and architects in Italy are in charge of only 25% of the total built volume of buildings … so there was little work for these professionals'. The Italian 'furniture industry' had only two firms with more than 500 employees, while its many small independent craft workshops allowed 'an ample margin of little experiments'.[26] Natalini calls this the 'theory-practice-theory check' that arose in this special condition of craft production in Italy and the overheated intellectual atmosphere of the period. But this 'overheated atmosphere' began to play itself out by about 1972, when the Radicals were put on an international stage at the Museum of Modern Art in New York for the exhibition 'Italy: The New Domestic Landscape'.[27] In addition to being included in this seminal exhibition, Superstudio continued to produce key works that year, as well as help co-found the short-lived open educational experimental workshop project Global Tools. Intended to be a revolutionary institution, it hoped to integrate education into the daily life of the population. This workshop was intended to be 'devoted to the formation of a school in Florence to nurture the creative facilities of every single human being and bridge the alienating gap that has taken the form between the work of the hands and that of the brain', and 'behaviors and gestures whose mere memory risks being erased by the logic of specialization, speed, and economic efficiency which characterize advanced capitalism'.[28]

This penultimate attempt by Superstudio in the Global Tools collaborative to reform the profession, brings us back full circle to the current practice of corporate architecture and the concentration on computer algorithms so prevalent in design practice today. The Florentines' call to nurture the creative facilities of human beings 'stifled by specialization and the frenzy to achieve efficiency' perfectly describes the working conditions of today's digital design environment.[29] If we fixate on Superstudio's compelling graphic images and ignore their social conception of labour and working, we miss the truly 'radical' nature of their project. It is imperative that the contemporary generation of critical practitioners continue to reform the meaning of work and labour begun by the Radicals nearly five decades ago. ⌀

Notes

1. Peter Lang and William Menking, *Superstudio: Life Without Objects*, Skira (Milan), 2003, p 31.
2. Patrik Schumacher, *The Autopoiesis of Architecture, Volume 1: A New Framework for Architecture*, John Wiley & Sons (Chichester), 2011.
3. See https://architecture-lobby.org and http://whobuilds.org/.
4. Mario Carpo, 'Post-Digital "Quitters": Why the Shift Toward Collage is Worrying', *Metropolis*, 26 March 2018; www.metropolismag.com/architecture/post-digital-collage.
5. *Casabella*, no 367, 1972. There is debate about when the term 'Radical Design' was first used. I refer to its use in *Casabella*.
6. Email exchange with Sam Jacob, 13 November 2018.
7. Email exchange with Jacopo Costanzo, 19 November 2018.
8. *Ibid*.
9. Email exchange with Benjamin Foerster-Baldenius, 13 November 2018.
10. Lang and Menking, *op cit*, p 31.
11. *Ibid*, pp 31–51.
12. *Ibid*, p 44.
13. Manfredo Tafuri, 'Design and Technological Utopia', in Emilio Ambasz (ed), *Italy: The New Domestic Landscape*, exhibition catalogue, Museum of Modern Art (New York), 1972, pp 388–404.
14. Lang and Menking, *op cit*, p 44.
15. *Casabella*, no 367, July 1972, pp 16–26.
16. *Ibid*.
17. Paul Ginsborg, *A History of Contemporary Italy: Society and Politics 1943–1988*, Penguin (London), 1990, p 212.
18. *Ibid*, p 298.
19. Lang and Menking, *op cit*, p 39.
20. Marie Theres Stauffer, 'Utopian Reflections, Reflected Utopias: Urban Designs by Archizoom and Superstudio', *AA Files*, 27, 1994, pp 23–36.
21. Lang and Menking, *op cit*, p 40.
22. *Ibid*, p 46.
23. *Ibid*, p 40.
24. Email exchange with Maria Gloria Biocchi, 14 November 2018.
25. Lang and Menking, *op cit*, pp 46–7.
26. *Ibid*, p 60, quoting Adolfo Natalini.
27. Ambasz, *op cit*.
28. Valerio Borgonuovo and Silvia Franceschini, *Global Tools 1973–1975*, SALT (Istanbul), 2015, p 12 (originally published 1974); http://saltonline.org/media/files/globaltools_scrd.pdf.
29. Ibid.

Casabella, no 367, July 1972

The then editor of *Casabella* Alessandro Mendini, who was also the author of the cover illustration, made the magazine available for the Global Tools group to publish its manifesto of 'the rejection of work as a necessary condition to the recovery of a meditative civilization'.

Text © 2019 John Wiley & Sons Ltd. Images: pp 14-15 Courtesy of Poltronova; p 17(t) © Warehouse of Architecture and Research; p 17(b) © © raumlaborberlin/Victoria Tomaschko; p 18(t) ©Traumnovelle; p 18(b) Image courtesy Drawing Matter Collections. Copyright the Architect; p 19(t) Courtesy of Superstudio; p 19(b) © MAXXI National Museum of the XXI Century Arts, Rome MAXXI Architecture Collection; p 20 © Galerie Graz Universalmuseum Joanneum, Austria. Photo J. Koinegg/UMJ; p 21 © Mondadori Portfolio/Electa/Marco Covi

FUNCTION FOLLOWS FORM

Sarah Deyong

SOME AFFINITIES BETWEEN PURE ICONS, HARDCORE ARCHITECTURE AND OOO

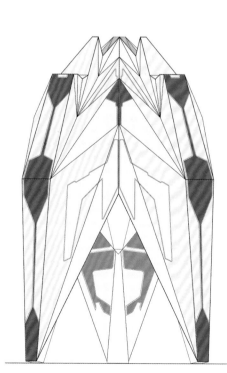

Inspired by late-Renaissance
still-life paintings, these large
light fixtures instantiate the
irreducibility of form to its many
fields: robots, tulips, lights.

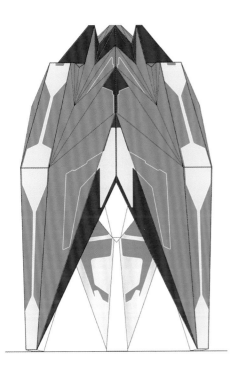
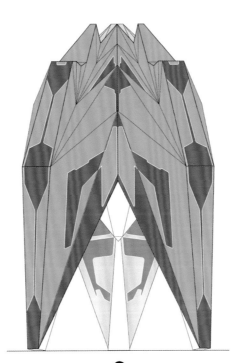
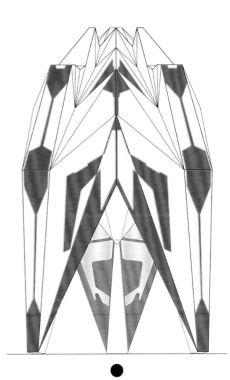

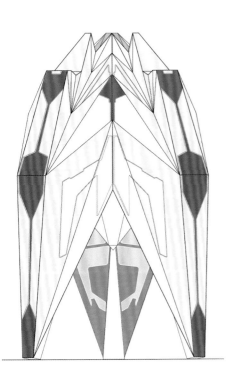
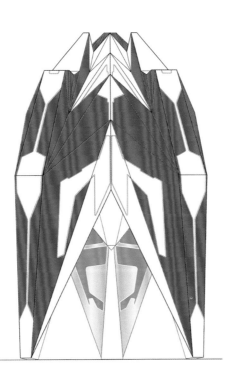
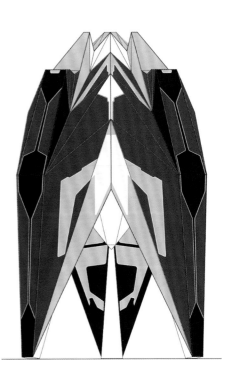

Sarah Deyong, an associate professor and director of the architecture programme at the University of Nebraska–Lincoln, maps the complex relationships contemporary theorists and practitioners have with concepts of 'form', which can be traced back to previous avant-gardes. She uses the work and publications of architectural collective WAI Think Tank as a microcosm of this complex discourse.

As history tells us, architectural ideas tend to cycle through periods. Mid-century, the dominant thinking was 'form follows function'. Circa 1968, the postmodern movement disrupted that formula. Whereas the dogmas of High Modernism foregrounded method, research and process at the expense of form, Postmodernism debunked the scientific rationale behind an all-too-simple functionalism. Instead it mined history's treasure trove of shapes, forms, figures and compositions, and found a taxonomy of building typologies. In eschewing design method, architectural theory decoupled itself from the rational methods of modern science and renewed its vows with architectural history. Specifically, it rewrote the terms of its engagement under the spectre of what Manfredo Tafuri denigratingly called 'operative criticism'.[1] Because the so-called operative critics – Bruno Zevi, Sigfried Giedion, Nikolaus Pevsner and Emil Kaufmann – had played fast and loose with history in order to promote the ideology of modern science, architectural theory strove for a more rigorous alliance with history while problematising all claims to truth.

And yet, there was a certain irony in recuperating building typologies. No matter how much one unpacked the 18th-century definition of typology – museums, theatres, prisons, hotels, banks and so on – a building's form was indelibly associated with its function, and hence, from a historical perspective, the roads still led to the artifice of this conjunction. Consequently, when it came to advancing a new position, it was the architect-theorist, rather than the historian, who proved particularly decisive. In his treatise *The Architecture of the City* (1966), Aldo Rossi gave typologies an ahistorical meaning. Reflecting on place, collective memory and the multiplicity of functions a building type like the Palazzo della Ragione (1219) in Padua has held in its lifetime, he succinctly argued that form was independent of function.[2]

The postmodern emphasis on form remains current to this day and has important implications for the discipline. For example, the recent work of Office Kovacs, and especially their Proposal for Collective Living (Chicago Architecture Biennial, 2017), underscores the importance of form in everyday life via the history of architecture.[3] This position effectively challenges the reactionary assumption that the primacy of form comes at the expense of function. In contemporary discourse, form is simple yet surreptitiously complex. On one hand, it is irreducible; its meaning is boundless. And on the other, form is projective; it harbours new agencies.[4]

While it may be too early to tell whether a paradigm shift towards a genuinely new approach to form has actually occurred, aspects of its various tendencies have already been documented on the pages of *Log* and *ARCH+*, for example, and the main protagonists have been recognised by enough of a critical mass to constitute a movement tied to the first two decades of the 21st century. As with all movements, the origins are many, but some of the more visible artefacts would definitely include Robert Somol's essays '12 Reasons to Get Back into Shape' (2004) and 'Green Dots 101' (2006);[5] Jimenez Lai's graphic novel *Citizens of No Place* (2010);[6] and the Possible Mediums project co-founded by Kristy Balliet, Adam Fure and Kyle Miller in 2013.[7] Tangent to this cluster is the group of architectural theorists associated with the philosopher Graham Harman and object-oriented ontology (OOO),[8] for example David Ruy, Mark Foster Gage, Tom Wiscombe and Todd Gannon. And coinciding with it is an array of early voices in Western Europe: François Blanciak's *Siteless: 1001 Building Forms* (2008);[9] the journal *San Rocco* (first issued in 2011); and Pier Vittorio Aureli's *The Possibility of An Absolute Architecture* (2011).[10]

Office Kovacs,
Proposal for Collective Living II
(Homage to Sir John Soane),
Chicago Architecture Biennial,
Chicago,
2017

The intention of the proposal was to 'make architecture from architecture'. In so doing, Office Kovacs appropriated the iconic section of Sir John Soane's House and Museum, replacing its contents, a collection of antique artefacts, with new objects from popular culture. The drawing therefore rehabilitates the neoclassical figure of the architect as a collector of exotic shapes and forms to posit a renewed stance on architectural form-making.

WAI Think Tank,
Understanding Pure Hardcore Icons,
London,
2013

Published in *Pure Hardcore Icons: A Manifesto on Pure Form in Architecture* (2013), this conceptual drawing depicts a romantic landscape of idealised building forms.

Architectural form (and its companion space) is not only irreducible to many fields, it is also central to the discipline's bid for alternative uses, programmes, narratives and agencies.

Hardcore Architecture

There are many entrances into this recent history of contemporary discourse, so the starting point of any narrative or line of thought is surely an arbitrary one. Here we will therefore begin with one of the lesser-known names, WAI Think Tank, founded in 2008 by Cruz Garcia and Nathalie Frankowski, whose appearance on the architectural stage bypassed the usual channels of legitimisation, as vetted by leading schools. Like the little magazines of the 1960s,[11] the first issue of their journal *What About It* (2011) was completely self-produced. But by actively promoting their ideas through their own publications, exhibitions and blogs, they made a place for themselves in academic discourse. They participated in the 'Archizines' travelling exhibition curated by Elias Redstone in 2012; the Shenzhen-Hong Kong Bi-City Biennale of Urbanism and Architecture organised by Aaron Betsky and Urban-Think Tank in 2015; and the first Chicago Architecture Biennial in 2015, at the invitation of Graham Foundation director Sarah Herda.

What had earned WAI's inclusion at these events was their manifesto statement on hardcore contemporary architecture, born in the aftermath of the economic crisis in 2008 in opposition to the massive proliferation of iconic buildings in cities like Dubai. However, WAI did not want to 'kill form', but to defend it from uncritical overuse. 'The paradox of contemporary architecture is that even though it doesn't have

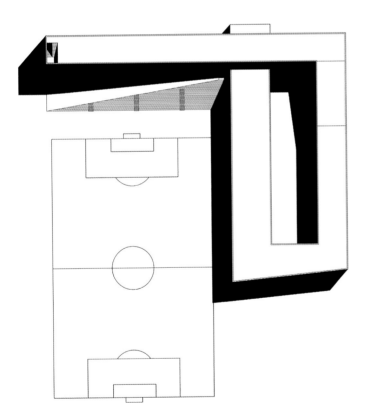

WAI Think Tank,
San Juan Football School and Training Center,
Puerto Rico,
2013

A single form integrates learning, living and training facilities in a boarding school to create a new model of educational institution focused on sports.

Blanciak Studio,
Pure Forms,
University of Sydney School of Architecture,
Design and Planning,
Sydney, 2012

The studio here reversed the conventional sequence of the design process. Instead of beginning with research, Blanciak's students began with an abstract form to find the building's function retroactively. Student work by Mingze Sun, Zoe Mairs, Rod Watt, Nicolette Quittner, Cameron Halls, Dong Hee Kim, Stephen Clement, Yang Lu, Chun Suh and Kanru Yang.

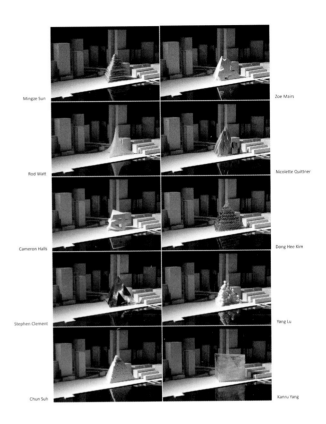

a written manifesto … it does have a shared visual language; an unclaimed plot,' they wrote.[12] In so doing, they turned to the history of the discipline – particularly the pure forms and 'abstract scrutiny' of Kazimir Malevich and the Russian Suprematists – in order to make a case for contemporary architecture's hardcore.

In their essay on 'The Shapes of Hardcore Architecture' (2011), WAI recalled an architectural event that encapsulates their thesis. That event was Peter Eisenman's presentation of his office tower for the Max Reinhardt Schauspielhaus in Berlin in 1992 to 'a battalion of … critics of intimidating gravitas', including Rem Koolhaas, who was not convinced by Eisenman's arguments, but had nevertheless found the looping form of his tower to be unspeakably beautiful. As we know, 10 years later, as WAI write, Koolhaas redeployed the looping form in his project for the CCTV building in China. They thus conclude: 'The reappearance of the looping skyscraper reinforce[s] the idea that a tower could be done as a Moebius strip and, more importantly, that after the abolition of concepts like scale, function, site or program, architecture can assume any shape in any place.'[13] Here we see an echo of Rossi's notion of pure forms independent of their function, with the caveat that contemporary architecture does not limit its formal investigation to platonic solids, but wilfully expands on their abstract possibilities.

In this series of drawings, architecture is
abstracted from the particularities of site,
context and programme to celebrate the
primacy of form and its endless diversification.

In this, WAI's 'hardcorism' is preceded by Somol's aforementioned essays, as well as by Blanciak's *Siteless*.[14] A common origin is the larger Dutch context of progressive practice and its sphere of influence on the Continent (here one thinks of the large collection of icons on BIG's homepage or Koolhaas's boozine *Content*, which featured Somol's 2004 essay). Paralleling WAI's own desire to 'explore the potential of architecture's infatuation with form', Blanciak similarly contends that 'the exhaustion and exacerbation of architectural form could not be achieved without a certain acceptance of form as a primary component of architecture'.[15] This view, he further argues, challenges the design process conceived as a linear investigation where form is narrowly and erroneously construed as a direct product of one's preliminary research (data-driven architecture and evidence-based design). In teaching design studios, Blanciak breaks with the typical project pattern of 'programme-plus-site-equals-form', and reverse-engineers this design formula. He says: 'This is where the intention of the studio connects with the *modus operandi* of *SITELESS*, as this traditional sequence is inverted in the brief; we start with form, then site, and the programme is to be determined through the project. Hence, the project becomes a tool for analysis.'[16]

Other affinities did not go unnoticed in academic periodicals, and in 2014 the Berlin journal *ARCH+* published WAI's work alongside that of Baukuh, OFFICE Kersten Geers David Van Severen, and Dogma (Pier Vittorio Aureli and Martino Tattara), whose members are all affiliated with *San Rocco*. The editors of *ARCH+* had originally chosen the theme 'New Postmodernists' for their double issue, but then changed it to 'Hardcore Architecture', and in recognition of the original source, featured WAI's collages on its covers.[17] This change was fortuitous, since the notion of form constituting the discipline's hardcore spoke less about historical influences à la

Postmodernism, such as Claude-Nicolas Ledoux and Étienne-Louis Boullée, and more about a shared insight into the very act of design, an insight which, in Blanciak's view, potentially reverses the failed equation of form follows function to function follows form.

The Irreducibility of Form to its Many Fields

In contemporary discourse, there are two positions that advance this insight, albeit in strikingly different ways. The first is Aureli's consideration of an absolute architecture, and the second, object-oriented ontology. The point of this comparison does not rely so much on the projects associated with these viewpoints as on their respective notions on the autonomy of form, or in the case of the latter, the autonomy of the object. Whereas Aureli promotes a productive tension between architectural form and its urban context,[18] Graham Harman speaks of the tension between the object and its sensual and affective qualities, and Todd Gannon, a sympathetic critic of OOO architecture, of the tension between abstraction and legibility.[19] Regardless of the category – context, sensual affect or meaning – all seem to recognise that architectural form, its *raison d'être*, cannot be reduced to a field of relations, be it epistemological or phenomenological. And in OOO, this orientation is indebted to Martin Heidegger's notion of tooling in *Being and Time* (1927).[20] Drawing on Heidegger, Mark Foster Gage, for example, offers a concise definition of OOO directed at an architectural audience, which, in turn, informs works such as Valentine to Times Square (2009) and Robotic Tulip Lamps (2010) – projects that are very much about the discipline of architecture and its internal dialogue with abstract form, rather than with function and meaning.[21]

According to Heidegger, the absolute unknowability of a form is instantiated when a tool, like a hammer, breaks down. The hammer is no longer a tool for driving nails;

WAI Think Tank,
Pyramid City on the cover of the ARCH+
double issue on Hardcore Architecture,
spring 2014

Conceptual collage of pyramidal buildings such as Buckminster Fuller's
Tetra City (1966), IM Pei's Louvre, Paris (1989), Norman Foster's Palace of
Peace and Reconciliation in Kazakhstan (2006), and MVRDV's renovation
of the Enver Hoxha Museum in Albania (2018).

it withdraws, and as such becomes available for other things, like a doorstop (even though it is not a doorstop). When form is understood solely in terms of use, it is, in the words of Harman, overmined; and when it breaks, stops functioning, then its strangeness or unknowability appears. This unknowability and changeability are what compels us to return to it repeatedly. Paradoxically, then, it is because architectural form is irreducible to function, context, meaning, affect and so on that it is constantly redeployed. For Harman, moreover, not only is form unknowable ('any attempt to get at form is an approximation'), so is space, for 'it is never what is directly present'.[22] Indeed, space is implied only through the presence of something else, and in architecture it is usually inferred by way of composition, as in a figure-ground or Boolean split. As such, one might think of architectural form (and its companion, space) not only in terms of its irreducibility to many fields (hammer, doorstop, robot, tulip, lights, chair, house), but also in terms of an iterative logic that asserts the primacy of form in support of architecture's bid for alternative uses, programmes, narratives and agencies. ∆

Notes

1. Manfredo Tafuri, *Theories and History of Architecture* [1968], trans Giorgio Verrichia, Harper & Row (New York), 1980, pp 141–70.
2. Aldo Rossi, *The Architecture of the City* [1966], trans Diane Ghirardo and Joan Ockman, MIT Press (Cambridge, MA), 1982, p 29.
3. See Dora Epstein-Jones and Bryony Roberts (eds), *Log: The New Ancients*, 31, Spring/Summer 2014.
4. Sarah Whiting, 'Whatever Happened to Projective Architecture?', *Footprint*, 3/4, January 2009, pp 123–8.
5. Robert Somol, '12 Reasons to Get Back into Shape', *Content*, Taschen (Cologne), 2004, pp 86–91, and 'Green Dots 101', *Hunch*, 11, Winter 2006–07, pp 28–37.
6. Jimenez Lai, *Citizens of No Place*, Princeton Architectural Press (Princeton, NJ), 2010.
7. See https://possiblemediums.wordpress.com, and also Matt Shaw, 'Possible Mediums', *Domus*, 19 February 2013: https://www.domusweb.it/en/architecture/2013/02/19/possible-mediums.html and Kelly Bair *et al* (eds), *Possible Mediums*, Actar (Barcelona), 2018.
8. See Graham Harman, *Tool-Being: Heidegger and the Metaphysics of Objects*, Open Court (Chicago, IL), 2002.
9. François Blanciak, *Siteless*, MIT Press (Cambridge, MA), 2008.
10. Pier Vittorio Aureli, *The Possibility of an Absolute Architecture*, MIT Press (Cambridge, MA), 2011.
11. On the little magazines of the 1960s and 1970s, see Beatriz Colomina and Craig Buckley (eds), *Clip, Stamp, Fold*, Actar (Barcelona), 2011.
12. Cruz Garcia and Nathalie Frankowski, 'The Shapes of Hardcore Architecture', *What About It?* (Beijing), 2011, p 21.
13. *Ibid*, pp 21–2.
14. Cited in Cruz Garcia and Nathalie Frankowski, 'Interview with François Blanciak', *Pure Hardcore Icons: A Manifesto on Pure Form in Architecture*, Artifice (London), 2013, pp 66–73.
15. *Ibid*, p 68.
16. *Ibid*, p 69.
17. Sabine Kraft, Nikolaus Kuhnert and Anh-Linh Ngo (eds), *Hardcore Architecture*, ARCH+ double issue, Spring 2014.
18. Aureli, *op cit*, p ix.
19. Todd Gannon *et al*, 'The Object Turn', *Log, 33*, Winter 2015, pp 87–8.
20. Martin Heidegger, *Being and Time* [1927], trans John Macquarrie and Edward Robinson, Basil Blackwell (Oxford), 1962.
21. See Mark Foster Gage, 'Killing Simplicity', *Log, 33*, Winter 2015; reprinted in Mark Foster Gage, *Projects and Provocations*, Rizzoli (New York), 2018, pp 34–40.
22. Graham Harman, Deep Vista Conference at Texas A&M University organised by Gabriel Esquivel, 20 June 2018: https://www.youtube.com/watch?v=zsrC8AQhu9M.

WAI Think Tank,
Sphere City on the cover of the
ARCH+ double issue on Hardcore
Architecture,
spring 2014

The cover image pays homage to the iconic sphere in the work of Claude-Nicolas Ledoux, Étienne-Louis Boullée, Richard Buckminster Fuller, Renzo Piano and others.

Text © 2019 John Wiley & Sons Ltd. Images: pp 22–23 © Mark Foster Gage;
p 25 © Office Kovacs; pp 26, 27(l) © WAI Think Tank; p 27(r) © François Blanciak;
p 28 © François Blanciak; p 29 Image © WAI Think Tank. Courtesy of *ARCH+*

Ada Wilson, *Crap Nightclub*,
Architectural Association (AA),
London,
1981

Wilson's student project, developed under the supervision of Michael Gold, and inspired by a figure drawing based on Duane Hanson's sculpture titled *Supermarket Lady* (1969). Note the similarities between the figure – including her dress – and the elements of architecture.

Igor Marjanović

Avant-Garde in the Age of Identity

Alvin Boyarsky, the Architectural Association and the Impact of Pedagogy

Under the stewardship of its iconic chairman Alvin Boyarsky, the Architectural Association (AA) presided over a burgeoning of architectural avant-garde tendencies that encouraged tutors and students to expand their architectural vocabulary and outlook by embracing issues of sexuality and identity, as well as other art forms. St Louis-based architect, historian and academic **Igor Marjanović** explores this era.

The 'mid-Atlantic' type is well known: at his happiest one hour out of Heathrow Airport, but happier still to return to the peace and calm of London – a curious, laissez-faire metropolis with a largish and sometimes notorious expatriate population. But what of that much rarer 'mid-Himalayan' species, with his deep cultural imprint balanced by a hard-won independence?

—Alvin Boyarsky, *Kisa Kawakami: Plus Minus Box*, 1986[1]

Reflecting on the work of the Japanese-born architect Kisa Kawakami, Alvin Boyarsky contrasted the notions of Western and Eastern identities. Leaving aside the questionable notion of the 'mid-Himalayan species', Boyarsky's comment alludes to the importance of identity and amalgamation of international perspectives that marked his tenure as the chairman of the Architectural Association School of Architecture (AA) from 1971 to 1990. Throughout this period, the AA acted as an incubator of new practices that both mirrored the emerging global tendencies such as semiotics, phenomenology and poststructuralism, while at the same time creating its own form of neo avant-gardism through the work of AA students and faculty such as Zaha Hadid, Rem Koolhaas, Bernard Tschumi and Elia Zenghelis, to name just a few.[2] Deeply embedded in architectural education, their avant-gardism engaged a wide array of pedagogical, curatorial and publishing endeavours that often questioned architecture's subjectivity, namely the identity of people and spaces.

Boyarsky was not a stranger to such questions. While a graduate student of Cornell University in Ithaca, New York in the late 1950s, he wrote a thesis on Camillo Sitte (1843–1903) as a critique of modernist city planning, influenced by Cornell Professor Colin Rowe. Referencing the cultural critic Matthew Arnold (1822–1888), Boyarsky wrote about Hellenes and Hebrews as embodying two types of worldviews – a holistic, idealistic one, versus a more detailed, specific one – anticipating also Rowe's discussion of foxes and hedgehogs in his 'Collage City' essay.[3] Perhaps an echo of his own Jewish-Canadian background, this awareness of identity grew even further during his tenure at the University of Illinois at Chicago in the mid-1960s, where he was deeply affected by the Civil Rights movement. There, he collected ephemera of the Black Panthers, who opposed police brutality against the country's African American population and participated in sit-ins for Cambodia, protesting American involvement in wars abroad.

Concerned with political issues in the US and overseas, he increasingly led a peripatetic life on a transatlantic axis, fully aware of his own foreignness. I have written previously about how these feelings of *estrangement* ultimately flourished at the AA where Boyarsky gathered many *other* strangers, transforming it from a British to an international institution for a combination of pragmatic and conceptual reasons.[4] But here I turn to the AA's design work to tell another story, namely how this diverse assembly of strangers brought the questions of identity to the fore, thus becoming instrumental in the dissolution of the modernist meta-narratives and the formation of a novel avant-garde paradigm.

The Black Panther: Black Community News Service, 6 April 1970

Based in Oakland, California, and distributed internationally, this was the official newspaper of the Black Panther Party, which vehemently opposed segregation and police brutality through community activism and self-defence.

Alvin Boyarsky sitting-in for Cambodia, University of Illinois at Chicago, 1970

The gathering was organised in protest at the continued expansion of American military involvement in South East Asia.

People in Architecture

Boyarsky's pedagogical reform of the AA in the 1970s and 1980s included the expansion across all levels of the school of the so-called unit system – an AA brand since Principal EAA Rowse first introduced it in the 1930s. A series of topical design studios based on current issues and faculty interests – and often linked to their international backgrounds – these units promulgated multiple approaches to architecture, using diversity and difference as the main currency of their distinction. As a consequence, each unit tried to push architecture to its limits and to brand itself through a radically new visual language. One of the seminal Diploma Units of the 1970s, initially led by Tschumi and later by Nigel Coates, produced books, videos and live performances. This approach built upon Tschumi's own shows at the Artists Space in New York City and his collaboration with the curator Roselee Goldberg. In 1975, they organised an exhibition 'A Space: A Thousand Words' – including artists such as Daniel Buren, Braco Dimitrijević and Dan Graham – which used the lessons of performance and body art to question the normative use of spaces.[5] Consequently, Dereck Revington's student project *Alkahest* (1974–5) was a performance piece in an abandoned warehouse, inspired also by Japanese place-making rituals. 'The work attempts to extend the limits of both architectural language and methodology and to recapture that original lost sense of *identity* with our surroundings and with our creations,' wrote Revington.[6] In 1980–81, the students in Unit 10 made costumes based on their personalities, culminating in a performance called *Modern Life*. Duane Van Dyke wore a big poncho and 'like a bat he would emerge from his corner of the room'. His face covered in drawing, he was 'learning to use his own body as a source for an enriched handling of the elements of architecture' – a metaphor of a rapid, 'electric' life of the 1980s.[7] These performances questioned the empirical and generic nature of building function and representation of users, re-enacting new and unexpected ways of using space and one's own body.

Consequently, the human body became a primary site of architectural production, including in the work of Narrative Architecture Today (NATØ), a group of AA students and tutors led by Coates. Rather than 'professionalism', NATØ and its eponymous magazine embraced contemporary culture, influenced by London's punk and fashion scenes (as well as the city's budding nightclubs). Echoing the avant-garde samizdat magazines, NATØ used lived experience as the source of architectural pursuits. NATØ 2's cover page (1984) referenced buildings, fashion and film, including male models of 'Dress Apprentices' inspired by Derek Jarman's homoerotic films. Such imagery questioned not only the boundaries of architecture, but also gender and sexuality, envisioning a discipline that is open, playful and diverse.

This diversity of human bodies is perhaps most evident in Michael Gold's unit, whose signature project *People in Architecture* could be read as a critique of modernist representation of buildings, often devoid of people.[8] In contrast, Gold's students first selected an image of a person, slowly adding elements to it: a piece of furniture, an interior element, an exterior space. Ada Wilson's *Crap Nightclub* (1981) was inspired by Duane Hanson's life-size sculpture of

Duane Van Dyke,
Modern Life performance,
Diploma Unit 10,
Architectural Association (AA),
London,
1980-81

Van Dyke was a visiting student from the US and together with other members of the unit (under tutors Nigel Coates, Richard Padovan (in the background) and António Lagarto), he participated in a workshop that resulted in specially designed costumes and a performance at the AA directed by Portuguese theatre director Ricardo Pais.

His face covered in drawing, he was 'learning to use his own body as a source for an enriched handling of the elements of architecture' – a metaphor of a rapid, 'electric' life of the 1980s

NATØ,
no 2,
1984

An antidote to the contemporary Festival of Architecture organised
by the Royal Institute of British Architects, *NATØ*'s second issue
features 'Dress Apprentices', whose characters recall both the
history of the profession and the contemporary fashion-design
scene. The issue also includes *NATØ*'s proposal for an imaginary
house for the iconic gay film director Derek Jarman situated in an
abandoned industrial building.

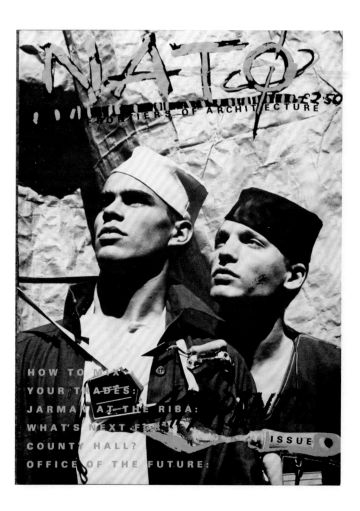

a *Supermarket Lady* (1969), featuring specific representation
of identity: race, age and sex. As such, the *Supermarket Lady*
could be seen as an antidote to Le Corbusier's 'Modulor'
(1945), an idealised albeit abstract representation of the
human figure and users of space. Subsequently, Wilson
designed a corporeal space made of soft, delicate fabric and
occasional body fragments – a space made both of building
and body components, all at once.

Lived Experience
Questions of identity also permeated Boyarsky's published
interviews with architects, which were a common feature
of AA catalogues. In his conversation with Hadid, he asked
questions about her identity and reception as a student at
the AA. 'I was seen as a wealthy Arab lady, waltzing in and
out,' she responded to Boyarsky and continued, 'I looked like
an actress between rehearsals, because I used to appear in
clothes I designed myself. I really resented being patronised.'[9]
Her self-designed garments reveal an awareness of identity
and difference – a very postmodern topic that was coupled
with Hadid's admiration for the modernist avant-garde. She
discovered Russian Constructivism through books and trips
to Moscow (and through her teacher Koolhaas, who admired
Ivan Leonidov). Consequently, *Malevich's Tektonik* was one of
her student projects and her later drawings often referenced
Constructivist imagery, with the ultimate goal of revisiting the
unfinished project of modernism. Her *Planetary Architecture
Two* catalogue from 1983 offers clues as to the finishing touch:
Kenneth Frampton wrote that Hadid's architectural geometries
resemble Kufic script, suggesting the merger of avant-gardism
with Hadid's Arab heritage.[10]

As the AA brought the historical and neo avant-garde
together, it allowed the latter to reinvent itself by means of
identity discourse, which also gradually substituted the social
agenda of modernism. Himself an admirer of Le Corbusier,
Boyarsky was also wary of those architects who assumed such
moral authority of an easily promised social change, many
of whom he initially encountered at the AA in the 1960s – a
school that 'was a *pink underwear scene*: a very lefty scene
on the one hand and on the other hand it was very much
a gentleman's club.'[11] This substitution of the revolutionary
colour red with the pinkish salon socialism parallels a larger
critique of the avant-garde at the time. In his *Theory of the
Avant-Garde*, Peter Bürger criticised the avant-garde's inability
to resist institutionalisation, but also noted the balanced
avant-gardism of German dramatist Bertolt Brecht (1898–
1956). Unlike the Dadaists, who sought to reject the institution
of art, Brecht, despite his disdain for capitalist theatre, sought
to change it, rather than discard it.[12] Boyarsky's work mirrors
this pragmatic approach – increasingly scrutinising the 'pink
underwear scene', he was also akin to the formal qualities of
the historical avant garde and to contemporary architects who
thought of themselves as such.

This pragmatic approach is also evident in the fact that
the AA promoted both speculative and built work, gradually
also merging questions of identity with avant-gardism. In his
1987 conversation with the Czech-born architect Eva Jiřičná,
Boyarsky asked questions about her background and Czech
Functionalism – one of the key modern movements of the
1920s and 1930s – as well as questions about her immigration

to the UK and her position as a female architect in a male-dominated field. Responding to Boyarsky, Jiřičná recalled a moment in the 1960s when she was assigned a job in a remote mining district of Socialist Czechoslovakia where her supervisor greeted her with a rude question, 'What am I going to do with a woman?'[13] Undeterred by such sexism, Jiřičná would move on to build her practice in the UK with buildings that fused the pre-Second World War Czech avant-garde tradition with the British high-tech. Throughout her AA catalogue, she is presented through these two lenses, but also through her own identity as a practising woman architect. This representation would influence the framing of her work beyond the AA: on the cover page of her later monograph *Design in Exile*, her face emerges behind a steel construction detail as if it were a mask.[14]

As student, faculty and visiting architects became increasingly comfortable and engaged with their own identity, they promoted what I would call a 'lived-experience avant-gardism'. Contrasting Manfredo Tafuri's criticism of the 'lifestyle avant-gardism' of the Dadaists and Surrealists, who dispatched new ideas from the autonomy and comfort of their 'boudoirs',[15] this lived-experience avant-gardism is infused with personal narratives and a high degree of externalisation through books, exhibitions and public events. It also mirrors larger societal discourses – including those on the diversity of human experiences, subjectivities and identities – resonating far beyond the confines of a single school and a particular moment in time.

Zaha Hadid at the Architectural Association (AA), London, 1975–6

Hadid is dressed in the clothes that she designed, sitting in the *Pink Room*, an installation by student Hans Hiegel (tutors: David Greene, Will Alsop and Warren Chalk).

Eva Jiricna: Design in Exile, 1990

Edited by Martin Pawley, this monograph (published by Rizzoli) tells the story of Jiřičná's architecture through a very personal story of immigration, difference and amalgamation of various cultural references: Czech and English, modernist and British high-tech.

Face, Space, Trace

Together, these documents, and those which are planned to follow, offer an insight into the range of conversations which have been taking place in recent years at the Bedford Square premises. That the pedagogical techniques invented have been able to trigger the energy and imagination of a *polyglot student body*, resulting in elaborate works of incomparable *diversity and depth*, should give heart to committed teachers and students elsewhere.
—Alvin Boyarsky, *People in Architecture*, 1983[16]

The externalisation of identity is exemplified here by Boyarsky's acknowledgement of the agency of the 'polyglot student body' to generate diverse and innovative work. Indeed, the school's premise made everyone feel at home: Arabs, Australians, Czechs, English, Japanese, Persians, South Africans and others. This community of strangers would become a powerful agent of the school's enduring legacy as its staff dispersed around the world, spreading its teaching ethos even into our own time.

As Dean of Architecture at Columbia University from 1988 until 2003, Tschumi recalibrated the school around the questions of representation – already explored through his AA unit – focusing on the emergent digital technologies and a prolific system of publications; Columbia's 'paperless studio' and the *Abstract* books were the hallmark of such reform. Another AA expat, South African-born architect Leon van Schaik, re-structured the programme at the Royal Melbourne Institute of Technology (RMIT) around practice-based research and a new doctoral programme inspired by the discursiveness and visual experimentation of the unit system.[17] Operating through global outposts in Europe and Asia, this programme allows practising architects to re-frame their work through advanced design research. Merging the roles of practitioners and scholars, the programme expands the identity of an architect beyond 'professionalism' (very much like the AA itself). *Serious Play: A Deltiology of Practice*, a doctoral dissertation by Nicholas Boyarsky – himself an AA graduate – frames his practice around his childhood in America and Europe and the playful influence of his father's postcard collection.[18] Dressed in working uniforms – referencing John Soane's drafting apprentices – the actors carried the drawings around as part of the dissertation defence, which was staged as a performance in an abandoned post office building.

The performative body of architects and the appropriation of abandoned spaces certainly echo the AA units, which continue to inspire the larger concept of design research – that is, research through drawing, making, practice-based scholarship and so on. In 1990, Peter Cook, a longstanding tutor at the AA, introduced the unit system at the Bartlett School of Architecture in London, thus influencing the next generation of educators. In 2015, Lesley Lokko – a graduate of the Bartlett's PhD by Architectural Design programme – launched the Unit System Africa at the University of Johannesburg Graduate School of Architecture (GSA), providing a contemporary platform for students and faculty to explore race and identity in a conceptually and visually sophisticated way. As they gather in yet another abandoned space – this time in the old Apartheid-era jails – the students are asked to draw upon the words and images that describe

Noir Radical, Volume², Summer 2019/19

FOLIO: Journal of African Architecture,
Volume 2: Noir Radical,
2019

Edited by Lesley Lokko and published by the Graduate School of Architecture at the University of Johannesburg, FOLIO showcases the pedagogy of the school but also design research more broadly, both from the African continent and its diaspora.

Dressed in working uniforms – referencing John Soane's drafting apprentices – the actors carried the drawings around as part of the dissertation defence, which was staged as a performance in an abandoned post office building their own identity. This projection of the subject is also evident in the GSA journal *FOLIO* – which recalls the AA Folios book series – where architectural patterns are overlaid on the portrait of a person, merging a face, space and traces of identity.

As the neo avant-garde architects embraced performance, representation and discourse, they probed the limits of their own subjectivity and of the entire discipline. It is perhaps an inherent aspect of human culture to discover another aspect of its own identity with each new epoch. The Civil Rights and Women's Suffrage movements brought issues of race and gender to the fore, as well as equity and access for all. And in our own moment – increasingly diverse but also polarised – identity remains an evolving territory where no individual is defined by a single experience but rather by multiple traces of many identities. As identity categories shift and expand – be it race, gender, ethnicity, age, social status, sexual orientation and so on – they allow architecture always to engage them anew, constantly expanding the field's subjectivity. And such is the enduring legacy of the lived-experience avant-gardism and of architectural education more broadly: to use one's own body as a site of architectural production and, ultimately, to embrace, engage and perhaps even change how we think about ourselves and the world around us. ⚤

Notes
1. Alvin Boyarsky, *Kisa Kawakami: Plus Minus Box*, Architectural Association (London), 1986, unpaginated.
2. The term 'neo avant-garde' is often used in distinction from the historical avant-garde of the 1920s and 1930s. Michael Hays uses the term 'late avant-garde' (in parallel to late capitalism): K Michael Hays, *Architecture's Desire: Reading the Late Avant-Garde*, MIT Press (Cambridge, MA), 2009.
3. Colin Rowe and Fred Koetter, 'Collage City', *The Architectural Review* 158, August 1975, pp 66–90.
4. Igor Marjanović, 'Alvin Boyarsky's Chicago: An Architectural Critic in the City of Strangers', *AA Files* 60, 2010, pp 55–78, and Igor Marjanović and Jan Howard, *Drawing Ambience: Alvin Boyarsky and the Architectural Association*, Kemper Art Museum and the RISD Museum of Art (St Louis, MO and Providence, RI), 2014.
5. Bernard Tschumi, 'A Space is Worth a Thousand Words', in Roselee Goldberg and Bernard Tschumi (eds), *A Space: A Thousand Words*, Royal College of Art (London), 1975, unpaginated.
6. Derek [sic] Revington, 'Alkahest', in Bernard Tschumi and Nigel Coates (eds), *The Discourse of Events*, Architectural Association (London), 1983, p 30 (my emphasis).
7. Nigel Coates, Richard Padovan and António Lagarto, 'Unit 10: Modern Life and the Impact of Architecture', *AA Projects Review 1980–81*, Architectural Association (London), 1981, unpaginated.
8. Michael Gold, *People in Architecture*, Architectural Association (London), 1983.
9. 'Alvin Boyarsky Interviews Zaha Hadid', in *Zaha Hadid: Planetary Architecture Two*, Architectural Association (London), 1983, unpaginated.
10. Kenneth Frampton, 'A Kufic Suprematist: The World Culture of Zaha Hadid', in *Zaha Hadid, ibid*, unpaginated.
11. Alvin Boyarsky interviewed by Bill Mount, 1980, unpaginated transcript, Alvin Boyarsky Archive, London (my emphasis).
12. Peter Bürger, *Theory of the Avant-Garde*, University of Minnesota Press (Minneapolis, MN), 1984, pp 88–9.
13. *Eva Jiricna: Designs*, Architectural Association (London), 1987, p 34.
14. Martin Pawley (ed), *Eva Jiricna: Design in Exile*, Rizzoli (New York), 1990.
15. Manfredo Tafuri, *The Sphere and the Labyrinth: Avant-Gardes and Architecture from Piranesi to the 1970s*, MIT Press (Cambridge, MA), 1987.
16. Boyarsky, *People in Architecture, op cit*, p 6 (my emphasis).
17. Leon van Schaik, *Mastering Architecture: Becoming a Creative Innovator in Practice*, Wiley-Academy (Chichester), 2005.
18. Nicholas Boyarsky, *Serious Play: A Deltiology of Practice*, doctoral dissertation, RMIT, 2016. Nicholas Boyarsky is the son of Alvin and Elizabeth Boyarsky.

Nicholas Boyarsky,
Serious Play,
doctoral dissertation defence,
Ghent,
Belgium,
2016

This practice-based research project, developed through the Royal Melbourne Institute of Technology (RMIT), included a grid of suspended architectural models and a performance with actors dressed as drafting apprentices carrying the physical drawings around the room. Left to right: Yoshifumi Hashimoto, Benjamin Boyarsky, Lorea Totorika and Elizabeth Boyarsky.

Text © 2019 John Wiley & Sons Ltd. Images: pp 30, 33, 35(t) © Architectural Association Photo Library, London; p 32 © Alvin Boyarsky Archive, London; p 34 © NATØ Group, Courtesy Nigel Coates; p 35(b) Courtesy Rizzoli New York; p 36 © Graphic Design: Fred Swart. Photograph: Alezkan Powell; p 37 © Nicholas Boyarsky

Stylianos Giamarelos

The Little Big Planet of Architectural Imagination

NEMESTUDIO, Re-Assembly
as Copper almost
demolished, New Cadavre
Exquis, 2017

Entering the materials life-cycle,
the originally digital objects turn to
physical ruins when demolished.
In this sense, materiality both
defines and undermines the
architecture of the archetypical
compositions.

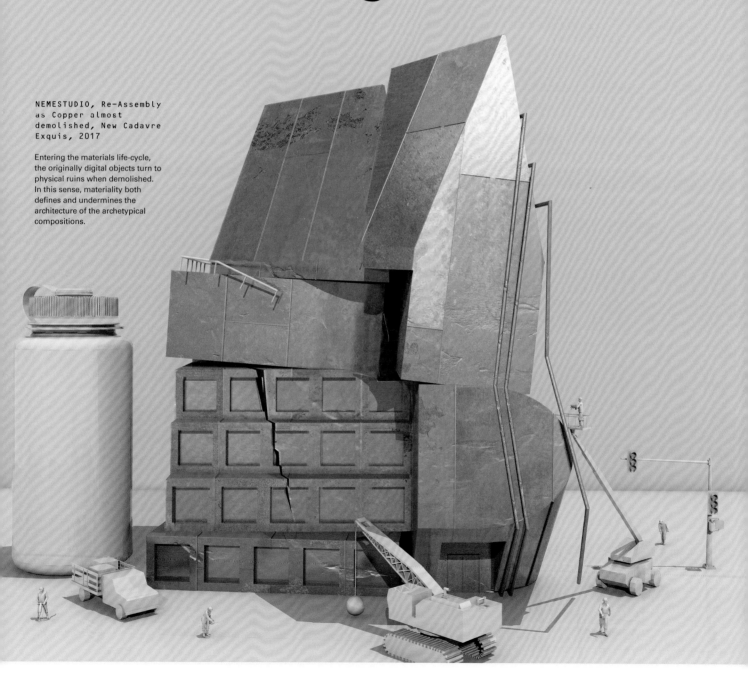

An Interview with NEMESTUDIO's Neyran Turan

NEMESTUDIO, Re-Assembly
as Copper, New Cadavre
Exquis, 2017

Random digital objects are re-
imagined and reassembled as
materialised architectural projects.
Upon gaining a material definition,
each reassembly obtains
architectural properties such as
scale and programme.

Informed by the radical Italian groups of the 1960s and 1970s, NEMESTUDIO's work addresses all manner of urbanisms in our time of 'Anthropocene' geomorphology, global warming and the temporality of construction materials. Architect, historian and theorist **Stylianos Giamarelos** interviews the San-Francisco-based practice's co-founder **Neyran Turan** to discover how the planetary scale of her thinking leads her back to the discipline of architecture and its history.

You know you are in the world of NEMESTUDIO when you look around you and see a diorama that foregrounds architecture's role in processes of deforestation, a section drawing of the earth across the Equator, an archipelago of single-material islands in their raw and architectural forms, and a crater on top of a decaying arcade. But the San Fransisco-based practice of Neyran Turan and Mete Sonmez is not limited to speculations such as these. Their projects not only look at the long shadow of architecture to explore its geographical and geological agency; through their form and content, they also reflect on the history of the discipline to reveal the many faces of the avant-garde architectural imaginary today.

The Political Architect

Before founding NEMESTUDIO in 2007, Turan and Sonmez studied architecture at the Istanbul Technical University. As an undergraduate student in the late 1990s, Turan recalls looking at the early drawings and projects of Zaha Hadid, OMA and Peter Eisenman: 'I don't think I fully understood the theory behind them then. But still, they showed me what an architectural model or a drawing could mean as an avant-garde practice.' Actively involved and intrigued by the political dimensions of architecture and urbanism, Turan decided to pursue these issues through her work.

This was an approach she carried forward during her graduate studies in the US. Keller Easterling's and Peggy Deamer's theory-focused classes at Yale University inspired her to develop her interests more systematically: 'I think that's when I first understood the work of Archizoom and Superstudio in the specificity of the Italian context. Their radical discussions and the critical/political interpretations of architectural urbanism served as a counterpoint to the techno-optimism of other avant-garde architects of the 1960s and 1970s.' Especially through Easterling's courses, Turan understood the international implications of her research questions. And her lasting interest in the expression of the political from within the discipline attracted her to Archizoom's representational stratagems: 'If you read the texts that go with Archizoom's frequently humorous or satirical drawings, their darker, critical side grows on you. They make you think about consumerism and capitalism through their specific attention to factories and shopping, and about how you might break that political cycle.' But this does not mean that their work moves away from architecture. As Turan explains, Archizoom offer another way to understand 'the relevance of architecture's history within these new contradictions. This was probably the first time I realised that widening your scope beyond the discipline actually meant looking back into it more rigorously.'

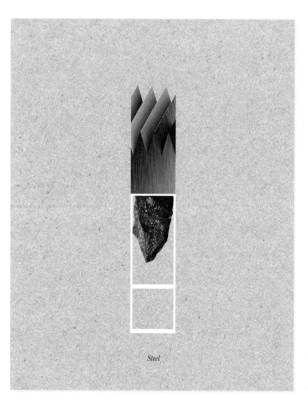

Steel

NEMESTUDIO,
Island of Steel,
Nine Islands: Matters
Around Architecture,
2016

The project re-imagines nine lavish or commonly used architectural materials as individual islands. The top parts of each island consist of the material in its architectural form, and the bottom parts in the raw form.

The Architectural Urbanist

The connection between Turan's work and that of the Italian groups of the 1960s and 1970s is clearer for her now: 'These radical groups challenged the idea that urbanism is always limited to the city. Industrial zones might have been understood as part of the urban, but Archizoom interpreted these spaces as urbanism in themselves.' Focusing on oil extraction in the North Sea, her thesis at Yale expanded the implications of this understanding along similar lines: 'My studies of energy landscapes showed how the sea became a kind of territory, geometrically mapped and partitioned by the countries around it. This was geography, it was mapping, it was territory, and so, I argued, it should be urbanism as well.'

During her doctoral studies at Harvard University's Graduate School of Design, Turan turned these ideas into a new theoretical framework. Her focus on geography, however, did not mean she left her previous training as an architect behind: 'Understanding the role of geography in relation to urbanism was not just meant to expand the field. I was really interested in the production of architectural knowledge through this kind of thinking. History, landscape and urbanism unexpectedly reinforced my interests in architecture as a discipline.' This strong grounding of Turan's work on the specificities of the architectural discipline distinguished her approach from concurrent debates about interdisciplinarity: 'I believe in architecture, and all these figures of the 1960s and the 1970s were also very serious about the ways they wanted to understand or change it. So I thought there was value in bringing these geographic and environmental discussions back into the architectural discipline in similar ways.' In addition, she found that these histories could inform her architectural imaginary in the present: 'Along with Archizoom and Superstudio, I also studied Oswald Mathias Ungers's work from the 1970s. These architects' work on the mega-form, on the role of architectural form in urbanism, was most relevant for my practice. Many of my early projects developed from these earlier approaches to architectural urbanism.'

The Geographic Architect

The projects Turan undertook as a practitioner and teacher in the architectural milieu offered her the opportunity to explore her theories on urbanism in new ways: 'I started to develop novel ways of thinking about making things. Focusing more on projection and imagination, a project would suddenly make me see things differently.'

In 2016, NEMESTUDIO accepted an invitation from co-curators Mark Wigley and Beatriz Colomina to contribute to the Istanbul Design Biennial. Titled 'Are We Human?', the brief asked participants to rethink what it means to be human in the age of the Anthropocene, the new human-made geological layer of the earth. Turan 'wanted to focus on something supposedly non-architectural that would somehow produce a collision with architecture'. The resulting Nine Islands: Matters Around Architecture project studied architecture's materiality from the standpoint of geography and geology: 'In this project, the materials we use in construction suddenly acquire an unfamiliar meaning just because they come from elsewhere. Commonly used architectural materials like marble are extracted, transported from the mine to the various supply chains of processing facilities, to the building site, before they eventually get demolished.' This long sequence in turn highlights scales that architects tend to ignore, namely 'the spatial scale of geography and the temporal scale of geology (the time it takes for materials to decompose, sometimes in cycles of 500 years)'. Understanding that architecture is necessarily enmeshed in these wide-spanning scales in space and time gives rise to a demand for a different course of action: 'I wanted to question this process, which unfolds on a planetary scale from the mine to the building, to see exactly what we do as architects in our material practice. There is so much we don't see in the piles of matter and "stuff" that is just there.'

Turan's latest book project[1] thus studies architecture's relationship with the planet we all share from our different geographic locations: 'It invites a planetary imaginary beyond environmentalism and technological determinism that addresses climate change not as a technical problem, but

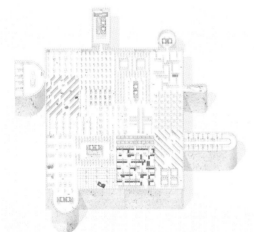

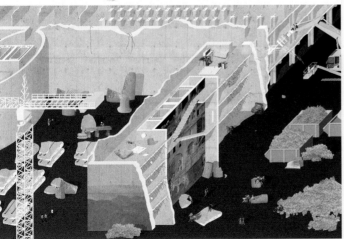

NEMESTUDIO,
Concrete,
Nine Islands: Matters
Around Architecture,
2016

Demolition is not only part of the long life-cycle of an architectural material, it is also part of architecture's longer geographic and geologic agency, which is constantly overlooked.

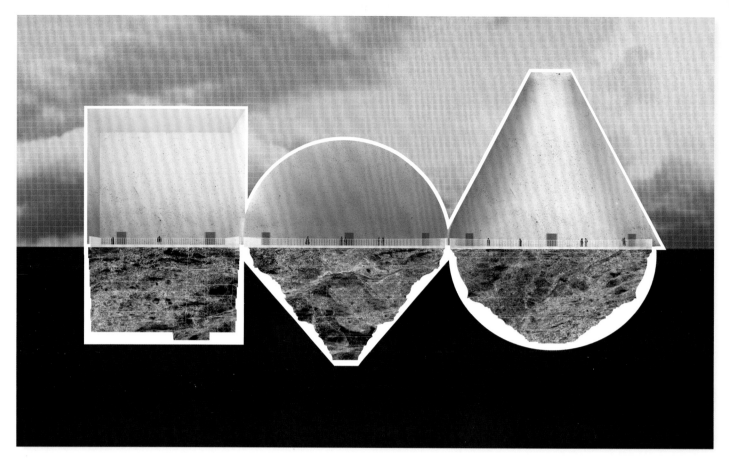

NEMESTUDIO,
Cenotaph for Rare Earth,
Museum of Lost Volumes,
2015

In this speculative geo-architectural fiction, the Museum of Lost Volumes raises public awareness around resource depletion of the 17 rare-earth minerals used for the production of green technologies.

as a cultural and political source that can be shaped by our discourses and representations. Architecture can serve as a measure for this imagination.' Implementing this planetary framework might be one of the greatest challenges for architects today, especially in relation to climate change: 'It's important to be able to act on this front, to get our hands dirty and to question many things about what we do. This might extend to the building codes that perpetuate our current practices of shaping the environment. All these things are integral to building.'

The Speculative Architect

However unfamiliar it may seem to most practising architects, Turan believes that this broader planetary framework also needs to challenge the ways in which they represent their work. NEMESTUDIO's acclaimed Museum of Lost Volumes (2015) started to develop this idea further. It was originally submitted to a competition on storytelling through architecture: 'The Museum of Lost Volumes was a good opportunity to test my ideas out visually. I wanted to show how architecture can talk about resource extraction through its drawing conventions. So I ended up designing spaces that look like a Natural History Museum.' But rather than looking at the dinosaurs or the many species that are now extinct, visitors to these museum spaces instead witness the remains of resource extraction in different geographic locations: 'In this project, the idea of the architectural section was juxtaposed with the geological section of the earth to demarcate the volumetric aspect of rare-earth mines. Looking back at my work now, I think this was a very important moment, where I developed my own voice through my practice.'

The Museum of Lost Volumes was a good opportunity to test my ideas out visually. I wanted to show how architecture can talk about resource extraction through its drawing conventions

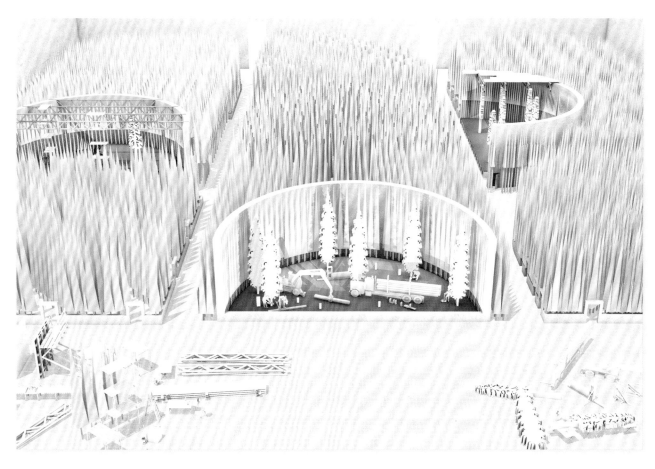

NEMESTUDIO,
Theatres of Deforestation,
Middle Earth: Dioramas for the Planet,
2017

In this diorama, architecture becomes a measure for the process of deforestation in Brazil and Indonesia, around the zero degrees latitude.

NEMESTUDIO,
Plastic Pacific Hall,
Middle Earth: Dioramas for the Planet,
2017

Current issues of climate change here become challenges for architectural representation. This diorama of an imaginary museum space gives architectural scale and proportion to the problem of plastic waste in the Pacific Ocean.

I wanted to imagine the material potential of these discarded models in the digital space. Once endowed on these initially digital objects, the material properties would then lead to their decay

NEMESTUDIO,
Sample Collection from the Earth,
New Cadavre Exquis,
2017

A random accumulation of digital three-dimensional models from the 3D Warehouse online platform, ranging from everyday objects, to building elements, primitive forms and natural features, are the raw ready-made materials for this architectural project.

Turan's newfound voice speaks in terms of a speculation that rests on theoretically rigorous and historically informed grounds: 'Speculative fiction became increasingly important in the projects I did at NEMESTUDIO afterwards. Middle Earth: Dioramas for the Planet [2017] expands on the ideas of the Museum of Lost Volumes, which carried similar representational ambition, but this time they are explored through the artefact of the diorama.'

In the New Cadavre Exquis project (2017), Turan encompassed the digital realm in the wide-ranging scope of her interests: 'It all started from the juxtaposition of the digital 3D Warehouse, an online garbage heap of open-source three-dimensional models, with the plastic waste collecting on Henderson Island in the Pacific Ocean'.[2] Turan re-imagined the objects of the 3D Warehouse as randomly assembled digital waste similar to the plastic heaps on the island shore. She worked with pieces from the digital heap to combine them in a series of uncategorisable architectural objects. But she was not only interested in the formal contradictions produced by the combination of unrelated objects: 'I wanted to imagine the material potential of these

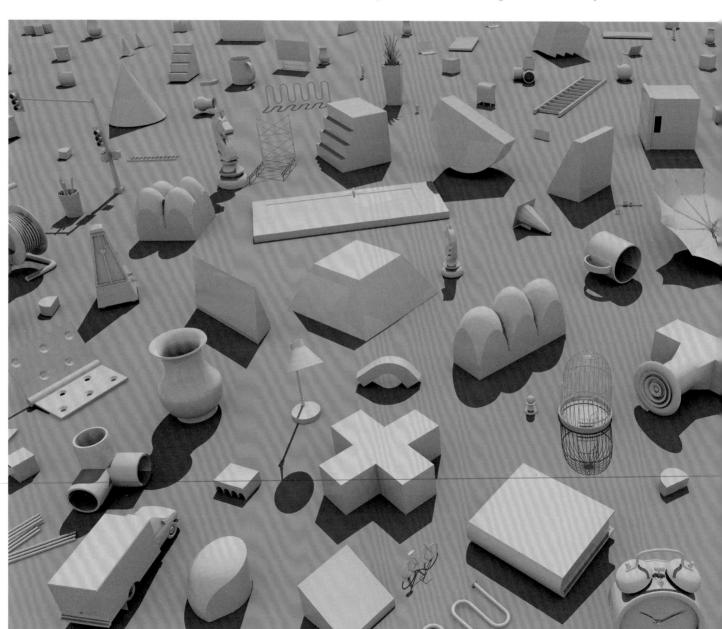

discarded models in the digital space. Once endowed on these initially digital objects, the material properties would then lead to their decay.' Her work suggests that in the era of climate change, discussions of the digital can no longer be dissociated from its material infrastructure. However, the project not only enabled her to study human junk in both the material and the digital domains: 'By depicting the formation of an architectural project starting from the accumulation of digital debris from the 3D Warehouse to its eventual transformation into a material ruin, the project re-staged the making of digital images as part of architecture's materiality.'

The Avant-Garde Architect

Working on such speculative projects has not only helped Turan clarify her affinities with the work of the avant-garde architects of the 1960s, she also now understands what kept their practices apart: 'Architecture as a discipline is obviously very different now in relation to its constituencies. The discipline can no longer choose between autonomy or engagement. Inside and outside have both collapsed.' Her work thus aims to respond to a different set of questions

altogether: 'The problem lies in building nuanced relationships between the wide-spanning scales in space and time that form part of the architecture. Although it tremendously benefited from the radical groups of the 1960s, my work in the fields of geography, geology and the environment has also now moved beyond them.' However, there are still some ways in which the avant-garde projects of Archizoom, Superstudio and their contemporaries continue to redefine speculative architecture: 'I still feel a connection to these groups in the sense that their work felt un-categorisable. The beautiful thing about the 1960s and 1970s was the creation of new categories of architectural projects, and thus new ways of thinking about architecture and the production of knowledge.'

These projects are unavoidably embedded in the politics of their time, and this is reflected in their creators' obsession with the vicious circle of industrial labour and consumption. But Turan still finds inspiration in the ways in which they chose to represent the real problems of their societies as architects: 'If you look at Archizoom specifically, there is an overload of the real in their work. They were not necessarily interested in producing an object, but in making this overload of the real visible. This obliges the viewer to reconsider their perception of architecture and its relation to the world.' Aimed at creating a similar effect, many of Turan's recent projects push this original quest for the excessive visibility of the real forward. However, this is not the only way she incorporates lessons from Archizoom in her current work: 'Archizoom's critical project is situated somewhere between architecture and the broader world. But for them, still calling this an "architectural" project was as important as their critique of capitalism, consumerism and the unprecedented build-up of the city.' This is how their work retains its pertinence today. Turan finds them especially inspiring 'when thinking about alternative relationships between the material and the representational to escape from the current reduction of architecture to mere problem-solving. Yes, things are different now, but these projects are still important to think about new ways to position our work, both in the discipline and in the world.' And there is certainly ample space for it all in the 'little big planet' of architectural imagination that Turan and NEMESTUDIO so thoughtfully explore. ᗐ

This article is based on a conversation between Stylianos Giamarelos in London and Neyran Turan in San Francisco conducted over Skype in November 2018.

Notes
1. Neyran Turan, *Architecture as Measure*, Actar (Barcelona), 2019.
2. Jennifer L Lavers and Alexander L Bond, 'Exceptional and Rapid Accumulation of Anthropogenic Debris on One of the World's Most Remote and Pristine Islands', *Proceedings of the National Academy of Sciences of the United States of America*, 114(23), June 2017, pp 6052–5.

Text © 2019 John Wiley & Sons Ltd. Images: pp 38-9, 40-45 Courtesy of NEMESTUDIO; P 39 (inset) Courtesy of Neyran Turan

FEEDBACK
OR, PAST FUTURES HAUNT

UrbanLab,
Re-Encampment,
Chicago Architecture Biennial,
Chicago,
2017

The architects translated a Superstudio photo-collage into a model that mimics the expansive grid with the use of mirrors. The infinite space is equal parts landscape and infrastructure.

LOOPS
ARCHITECTURE'S PRESENT

Mimi Zeiger

Is architectural discourse haunted by an avant-garde future that never materialised? Los Angeles-based critic, curator and editor **Mimi Zeiger** describes how these tropes, many of which relate to the preoccupations of the 1960s and 1970s, are recycled and repurposed by contemporary practitioners. She cautions that such feedback loops, orbits or revolutions strip meanings, narratives and politics from original source materials, which not only leaves a vacuum of nostalgia at the centre of the discourse, but also limits the discipline's ability to speculate on the pressures of our present moment.

In February 2018, Elon Musk's SpaceX launched a cherry-red Tesla Roadster into the heavens perched atop a Falcon Heavy rocket. Equal parts media stunt and feat of technological prowess, the act epitomised the very near reality of entrepreneurial space exploration.

Cruising past Mars and travelling at speeds reaching 56,000 kilometres (35,000 miles) per hour[1] brings to mind the velocity celebrations of a century earlier when Futurist Filippo Tommaso Marinetti wrote: 'We are already living in the absolute, since we have already created eternal, omnipresent speed.'[2] But while the avant-gardist Marinetti eschewed the past's crepuscular sentimentality, techno-futurist Musk's 21st-century sports car carries cultural baggage from the mid-20th; a dummy pilot named Starman is seated in the Tesla's front seat 'listening' to an infinite loop of David Bowie's 'Space Oddity'.

LOOP I: ORBITS

Bowie's 1969 hit, of course, is a cautionary tale of the Jet Age – Major Tom helplessly adrift among the stars. Musk's soundtrack, then, must mean something more for our contemporary moment than baby-boomer pandering or glib nostalgia. It illustrates 'hauntology' – a condition of late modernity in which we long for promised futures, utopias or even avant-gardes that never arrived. Marinetti promised speed. The Jet Age promised off-world exploration. And yet we remain mostly terrestrial on a rapidly warming planet, haunted by old desires.

First coined by Jacques Derrida in his 1993 book *Spectres of Marx*, and elaborated on by theorist Mark Fisher more than a decade later, hauntology describes a kind of temporal feedback loop, where noise from the past interrupts the signal from the present.[3] In practice, the term makes sense of moments of expansive reach that are tempered by reflection. The legacy of Modernism's systems and structures lingers spectrally around mainstream culture and architecture, even as confidence in the project of modernity has long been shaken, questioned and rejected.

LOOP II: REVOLUTIONS

And 50 years after the riots and protests that marked the end of that old world order, we continue to also cling to counter cultures, radicals and revolutions. Writing about The Shed, a recently opened multimedia performance space by Diller Scofidio + Renfro with Rockwell Group, located on New York City's High Line, art historian Claire Bishop critiques the use of Cedric Price's Fun Palace (1964) as both inspiration and precedent.[4] Commissioned by theatre director Joan Littlewood, Price's unbuilt work proposed an adaptable and educational cultural centre that embraced the shifting social norms of British society. According to a brochure published by Price and Littlewood, it was conceived as a place to start a riot, begin a painting or stare at the sky, or to revolt, create or, most radical of all, do nothing.

The Shed is a technologically ambitious project distinguished by an enormous roof on wheels that moves

Diller Scofidio + Renfro
and Rockwell Group,
The Shed,
New York City,
2019

Located on the High Line, The Shed is
a cultural and performing-arts space in
Manhattan. Its large, retractable roof
takes inspiration from Cedric Price's
ever-mutable Fun Palace project.

Cedric Price,
Interior perspective
for Fun Palace,
1963

Commissioned by theatre
director Joan Littlewood,
Price's Fun Palace is a
favourite project for revisiting,
but is it possible to translate
its social and political
agenda from the 1960s to a
contemporary context?

to accommodate a highly curated set of performances and events. Bishop takes issue with the portrayal of Price's work in historian Dorothea von Hantelmann's 'What Is the New Ritual Space for the 21st Century?' booklet produced to accompany the venue's two-week preopening programme.[5] Specifically, Bishop identifies Von Hantelmann's reorientation of the Fun Palace from a piece of agit-prop theatre to a tool of contemporary consumer culture. She writes: 'It's a staggering rhetorical shift that takes up what is most proto-neoliberal in Price (the mantra of flexibility) and rebrands it as prosumerism.'[6]

The Shed opened in April 2019, and at the time of writing what little architectural discussion there has been about the project has focused on the Fun Palace. Price's vision has become a recursive figure that not only replaces discourse about the architectural gestures, but even when critiqued is a palliative that eases the reception of an uncomfortable new world order – in this case, a gentrified West Side of Manhattan fully optimised for the churn of capitalised art, culture and media.

As with Price, the work of Italian radicals Superstudio provides endless fodder for appropriation. Their signature black-and-white grid decorates tote bags, tunics and bedding produced by trendy, minimalist fashion brands. Quaderna, the anti-design tables and benches Superstudio created for furniture manufacturer Zanotta in 1970, pops up in chic cafes and design galleries. The flatness of its plastic laminate and the particular spacing of the silkscreened grid (3 centimetres/1.2 inches) make Quaderna an instantly recognisable visual reference. For example, OMA's 2016 adaptive reuse and renovation of Fondaco dei Tedeschi in Venice cheekily deploys the grid in the public bathrooms on the upper level. The use is knowing – an act typical of Rem Koolhaas and the OMA team who also worked on Fondazione Prada in Milan (2018). The question flickers: Is it an inside joke or a nod to contemporary design trends?

At Fondazione Prada, though, the references are fast and furious. The brashest is Restaurant Torre, a pitch-perfect near-re-creation of Philip Johnson's Four

OMA,
Fondaco dei Tedeschi,
Venice, Italy
2016

The uppermost floor of Fondaco dei Tedeschi is a skylight art and events space. Although grids play a role in the architectural vocabulary of the gallery, it is the use of a Superstudio-like grid in the bathrooms that suggests an Italian Radicals feedback loop.

Seasons restaurant (New York, 1959) on the sixth and seventh floors of the new tower, complete with electric-blue chairs bought at auction. Hauntological more than postmodern, the decor transfers an interior designed for mid-century power brokering into the nexus of global art and fashion.

At Fondaco dei Tedeschi,[7] the gesture is smaller and more oblique, though no less relevant. The historic building dates to the 13th century as a hub of trade, serving as a customs house under Napoleon and a post office under Mussolini. OMA's 2016 renovation transformed the structure into a duty-free shopping emporium for Hong Kong-based operator DFS. The uppermost floor is dedicated to an event pavilion, exhibition space and open-air rooftop offering a Venetian panorama. The public toilets on this level overtly reference a radical past: Superstudio's Quaderna graphic patterns the walls, backsplashes and stalls, creating a feedback loop to 1970s Italy and the anti-nostalgia impulses of the group.[8]

Johnston Marklee,
MCA Chicago,
2015

The architects collaged together Superstudio's trademark grid with the abstracted grid of the Museum of Contemporary Art's facade.

LOOP III: MATRICES

The degree to which Superstudio's efforts have become recognisable shorthand for avant-garde authenticity can be seen in a photo-collage produced by architects Johnston Marklee as part of their contribution to the 2015 Chicago Architecture Biennial. Entitled *House is a House is a House is a House is a House*, they later published a monograph with the same title. In the piece, the architects deploy a portion of *Continuous Monument* (1969) in this proposal for the city's Museum of Contemporary Art (MCA). The top half of the collage is an abstraction of the original 1996 building by Josef Paul Kleihues – a monumental stair leading to the facade and its oversized window grid. The bottom half was borrowed from Superstudio to serve as a stand in for urban life – the silhouette of a hippie couple holding hands as the monument's supersurface stretches outwards. In the original, the grid extends existentially towards its vanishing point; in Johnston Marklee's collage, however, the mediation on endless urbanity ends at the foot of the museum's steps.

While the architects' composition might suggest an interrelationship between culture and the city (an oft-told story at a time when museums around the world are trying to build greater audiences), the abrupt halt of the grid may tell us something more than what was intended: what had been open-ended, visionary and problematic is cropped and Photoshopped to serve the more straightforward architectural goal of pursuing a commission. That said, the reference is not decontextualised; meanings are meant to remain, not to give historical context per se, but to legitimate value.

Sharon Johnston and Mark Lee used a similar technique of leveraging historical material to validate the present on a greater scale in 2017 with their curatorship for the Chicago Architecture Biennial. Entitled 'Make New History' (a title taken from Ed Ruscha's artist's book of the same name),[9] the exhibition codified a trend of emergent designers to put precedents into architectural service. The catalogue includes a conversation between the architects and Graham Foundation director Sarah Herda on the merits of history. Herda asks Mark Lee if he considers the use of history a reactionary stance. Lee dodges the implications that history comes with disciplinary baggage or that looking backwards is wilfully regressive. Instead he suggests that our information age offers rich access to the past, creating an atemporal treasure trove for designers, an 'eternal present' of historical knowledge: 'Perhaps unlike historicism, where things are subsumed under a grand historical narrative structure, we see history as a horizon, open and accessible, with multiple entry and exit points.'[10]

LOOP IV: ETERNAL PRESENT

But what if the 'eternal present' is not an interstate freeway trucking across time and space, but rather a *Groundhog Day* scenario in which difference is subsumed by familiarity and repetition? The past can be a dangerous place to look for the future of architecture. Re-imagining the avant-garde might seem celebratory at first, but unless radically recontextualised and critiqued it can be a trap. Old biases and omissions are reinforced: canons crystallised, hierarchies hardened, patriarchal practices protected.

Johnston and Lee's 'Make New History' included a hall in the Chicago Cultural Center dedicated to 24 invited practices, each asked to contribute an interpretation of a canonical interior of their choosing based on a photograph. The selections of archival images were primarily of European architecture authored by men, an unsurprising consequence given tendencies in the field over its long history. The resulting models were laid out in a pattern representing Mies van der Rohe's 1947 masterplan for the Illinois Institute of Technology (IIT) campus – a pattern that when translated to the gallery was nearly illegible. A missed off-ramp – a gesture so reliant on a niche reference that when considering a broader Chicago audience borders on exclusionary.

Within this milieu, which included Bureau Spectacular's *Another Raumplan*, a furry interpretation of Adolf Loos's 1930s Villa Müller in Prague, and UrbanLab's Re-Encampment, their interpretation of Superstudio's 1971–3 *Fundamental Acts* (*Life*, *Education*, *Ceremony*, *Love* and *Death*) (see p 20), the different designers competed to

Bureau Spectacular, *Another Raumplan*, Chicago Architecture Biennial, Chicago, 2017

Another Raumplan used faux fur and a series of peepholes to pay homage to a photograph of Villa Müller, Adolf Loos's 1930s house built in Prague.

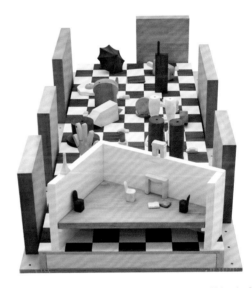

WELCOMEPROJECTS, *I See Paris, I See France*, Chicago Architecture Biennial, Chicago, 2017

By amplifying the Surrealism at play in Le Corbusier's Beistegui Apartment (1931), the playful project introduced a new set of narratives and references for architectural consideration.

stand out with a clever, recursive wink. Several used found and oddball-scale objects (Doritos bags, lawn chairs, cacti) to fill their dollhouse-like models.

WELCOMEPROJECTS's take on Le Corbusier's Beistegui Apartment (1931), entitled *I See Paris, I See France*, applied both rigour and whimsy to the challenge, transforming the rooftop penthouse into a Surrealist board game, with questions of scale and reality as the stakes. A Popsicle, a top hat, a lipstick, a fried egg are all players on a chequerboard surface – designed to defy distinctions between toy, object or, in postmodern duck fashion, building. In describing her project, WELCOMEPROJECTS founder Laurel Broughton reminds us that the apartment no longer exists and that only a handful of images are left behind: 'It is this status – a ghost captured in a photograph – that makes this work of architecture simultaneously real and imaginary.'[11]

LOOP V: SAMPLES

Though haunted, *I See Paris, I See France* does not rely on any single visual quotation for meaning. The apartment itself is only one of many objects on the board. Broughton, travelling in the path of Venturi, Scott Brown and FAT, among others, raises the possibility that extradisciplinary sources offer a critical exodus from the tyranny of the feedback loop and the traditional cannon.

Broughton's interconnected works *Life on the Fantasy Substrate of Los Angeles* (2018), a small booklet produced for an exhibition at the Cities of Days shop and gallery in Los Angeles in October 2018, and *Four Experimental Mascots for Los Angeles*, envision a future for LA circa 2026, in which the city is transformed into a citizen-operated theme park. Her speculative urbanism relies on collective referencing – Reyner Banham's ecologies[12] and history of buildings and neighbourhoods as hats, hot dogs or Venetian dreamscapes, but also collective labour. 'All citizens are now cast members and characters who contribute to the ongoing narrative of place. This promotes awareness that narrative is work. ... Uniforms are provided,' explains Broughton.[13] While Bishop's critique of The Shed, with its dubious embrace of Price's Fun Palace, cautioned against prosumerism – the neoliberal conflation of production and consumerism – Broughton's fiction is based on legislation and participation, on citizens voting to transform their city into a theme park.

Like Broughton, the work of Jennifer Bonner, founder of MALL, makes productive excursions into the ordinary. She drags enduring vernaculars of Southern culture – roof gables and faux finishes – from the fringes of Americana and reshapes them within the discipline. Bonner's methodology, as demonstrated in Haus Gables (2018), relies on a multistep process of sampling, repurposing and making strange. The gable roof, for example, is identified as outcast, reconfigured, and then re-represented using photographic techniques inspired by artist Barbara Kasten: oblique angles, multicoloured gels, deeply hued shadows.

MALL's interest is clearly form, but it is also driven by a desire to broaden the histories acceptable within the discourse. In her book *A Guide to the Dirty South – Atlanta* (2018), Bonner draws parallels between East Coast/West Coast rivalries in hip-hop and in architecture. As a way out of the feedback loop between Los Angeles and New York, she introduces a third coast: Atlanta, home of hip-hop collectives Outkast and Goodie Mob. 'Welcome to the Dirty South architecture camp, where a group of thinkers, writers, misbehaving makers, and storytellers borrow from Dirty South hip-hop artists before them to produce outcast architecture,' she writes.[14] The *Guide* is inclusive in its approach, including grand hotels by architect John Portman alongside landscapes drawn from rap lyrics.

MALL's interest is clearly form, but it is also driven by a desire to broaden the histories acceptable within the discourse.

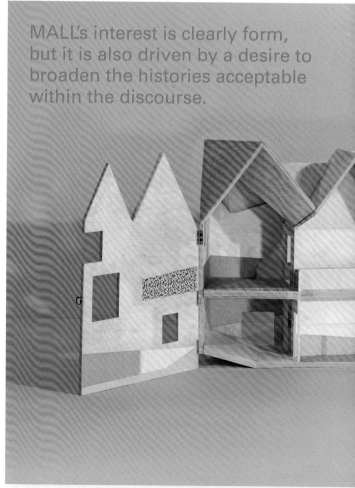

MALL,
Haus Gables,
Atlanta,
Georgia,
2018

MALL's formal language is drawn from the many vernaculars of the American South, including home construction and Dirty South rap. Multiple pitched roofs are designed to make the gable seem strange or unfamiliar.

WELCOMEPROJECTS,
*Four Experimental Mascots
for Los Angeles,*
2018

Within the speculative fiction of *Life on the Fantasy Substrate of Los Angeles*, a small booklet produced for an exhibition at the Cities of Days shop and gallery in Los Angeles in October 2018, citizens of the city don mascot costumes based on Reyner Banham's four ecologies, including Surftopia and Autotopia.

LOOP VI: CENTRIFUGAL FORCES

Architecture's capacity to imagine, or re-imagine, an avant-garde relies on its ability to move beyond the avant-gardes of years gone by. We might be tempted to continually look backwards, haunted by the embedded meanings of those tantalising projects of the 1960s and 1970s, but the rear-view mirror of history is narrow, framing a body of work that is often decidedly Western, male and white. Hence those pasts present only a crutch for a field struggling to find its relevance and for next generations of designers faced with increasingly complicated planetary conditions.

But not looking back is not all call for newness, either. Tabula rasa visions are just as limiting. Although still early in their careers, what the work of Broughton and Bonner suggests is that expansion into less-explored territories of politics and narrative, region and identity can not only coexist with more disciplinary agendas; they are crucial correctives to the centrifugal pull of the feedback loop. ∞

Notes
1. www.whereisroadster.com.
2. Filippo Tommaso Marinetti, 'Founding and Manifesto of Futurism', *Le Figaro* (Paris), 20 February 1909, published in Lawrence Rainey (ed), *Futurism: An Anthology*, Yale University Press (New Haven, CT), 2009, p 51.
3. See Andrew Gallix, 'Hauntology: A Not-So-New Critical Manifestation', *The Guardian*, 17 June 2011: www.theguardian.com/books/booksblog/2011/jun/17/hauntology-critical.
4. Claire Bishop, 'Palace in Plunderland', *ArtForum*, September 2018: www.artforum.com/print/201807/palace-in-plunderland-76327.
5. Dorothea von Hantelmann, 'What Is the New Ritual Space for the 21st Century?', May 2018: https://theshed.org/program/series/2-a-prelude-to-the-shed/new-ritual-space-21st-century.
6. Bishop, *op cit*.
7. http://oma.eu/projects/il-fondaco-dei-tedeschi.
8. Lucia Allais, *Designs of Destruction: The Making of Monuments in the Twentieth Century*, University of Chicago Press (Chicago, IL), 2018, p 263.
9. Ed Ruscha, *Make New History*, Museum of Contemporary Art (MOCA) (Los Angeles), 2009.
10. Sarah Herda, Sharon Johnston and Mark Lee, 'From the First Biennial to the Second and Back Again', in Mark Lee *et al*, *Make New History: 2017 Chicago Architecture Biennial*, exh cat, Lars Müller (Zurich), 2017, pp 21–2.
11. www.welcomeprojects.com/chicago-architecture-biennial/.
12. Reyner Banham, *Los Angeles: the Architecture of Four Ecologies*, introduction by Anthony Vidler, University of California Press (Berkeley and Los Angeles), 2001, p 5; originally published by Allen Lane (London), 1971.
13. WELCOMEPROJECTS, *Life on the Fantasy Substrate of Los Angeles*, Summer 2018: https://days-la.myshopify.com/products/life-on-the-fantasy-substrate-of-los-angeles?variant=8960342720572.
14. Jennifer Bonner, *A Guide to the Dirty South – Atlanta*, Artifice (London), 2018, pp 7–8.

Text © 2019 John Wiley & Sons Ltd. Images: pp 46–7 © Michelle Litvin Studio; p 49(t) Courtesy of Diller Scofidio + Renfro in collaboration with the Rockwell Group. Photography by Brett Beyer; p 49(b) © Cedric Price fonds, Canadian Centre for Architecture; p 50(t) Photo Delfino Sisto Legnani and Marco Cappelletti, Courtesy of OMA; p 50(b) © Johnston Marklee. Photo: the Art Institute of Chicago / Art Resource, NY; p 51(t) Courtesy of Chicago Architecture Biennial; pp 51(b), 52–3(t) Courtesy of WELCOMEPROJECTS; pp 52-3(b) Courtesy of MALL

ARCHI
OF
AFFINI

Office Kovacs,
Guggenheim Helsinki
Museum,
Helsinki,
2014

In this unsubmitted competition
entry, a highly differentiated field
of architectural compactions
are scattered throughout a
hypostyle hall, allowing for both
conventional and new ways of
experiencing and viewing art.

VE

MAKING ARCHITECTURE

Andrew Kovacs

FROM ARCHITECTURE

TIES

Archive of Affinities is a digital collection and display of architectural objets trouvés, created and curated by **Andrew Kovacs**, assistant adjunct professor at the University of California Los Angeles. Elements, forms and architectural notations are selected from the Archive's galaxy of possibilities as the *prima materia* for his practice's projects. The juxtaposition of scale, taxonomies, typologies and colour gives the work of Office Kovacs its own particular flavour.

In the Internet era, every image is an advertisement. Almost every architect contributes to the limitless overabundance offered by social media by sharing instantaneous personal archives, student projects and their own work. Each image is a miniature manifesto shared with the broader public, circulating freely and endlessly – they shape and identify the work of architects, they track and create lineages and alliances, and they also begin to form and transmit sensibilities, ideologies and aesthetic preferences, both individually and collectively.

Archive of Affinities is a contribution to this melee. In the early 2000s the Internet was a very different place than it is today. The beginnings of the project therefore required searching for images and saving them into an image bank on a hard drive, organised by architects' names and other loose themes. It evolved further at graduate school as a process of trawling through the libraries and scanning everything that appealed or was being researched for some purpose, typically as a resource for a student design project. By this time, old architecture books and magazines were super cheap. The bookstore was dying and the Internet was rising. Anything could be ordered from anywhere, and often sold and shipped for an inexpensive amount. Images from these books were scanned and uploaded onto a Tumblr site, still active today.

This was the context in which Archive of Affinities was created. It has no deadline, no client and no budget. Strictly speaking, there are multiple versions of its 'site' – an Instagram account, Tumblr blog, Twitter feed, and a single folder on a hard drive.

A Galaxy of Architecture

Archive of Affinities is a constantly updated collection of architectural images that exploits the dual meaning of affinity: personal predilection and the resonant relationship between images. If the canon of architecture is a solar system, Archive of Affinities strives to be a galaxy. If the canon is limited and exclusive, this is expansive and inclusive.

In many ways Archive of Affinities has become the source, originator and reference point of the work of Office Kovacs. At times the images shared relate to projects being worked on in the studio. At other times they are intended as references to be mobilised. Architectural drawings such as floor plans or sections eventually spark up new speculative projects. Plan for a 9 Square Grid (2012), for example, is made up of existing floor plans that have then be altered, adjusted and arranged into a new plan. This notion, that the material shared on Archive of Affinities is to be used as a catalyst for new projects, developed into an approach called 'Making Architecture from Architecture'. If architecture organises the world around us, then the aim of Making Architecture from Architecture is to evaluate that material and rearrange it for new architectural purposes. In other words, Archive of Affinities serves as a reservoir from which architecture from architecture can be made.

Making a Methodology

Mined from Archive of Affinities, each of the floor plans used in the creation of the Plan for a 9 Square Grid is the result of the accumulation and adjacency of multiple drawings

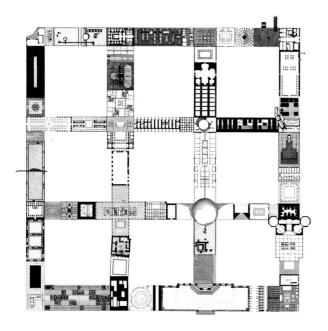

Office Kovacs,
Plan for a 9 Square Grid,
2012

Speculative proposal for a floor plan made up of floor plans collected as part of the Archive of Affinities project. The plans are fragments and wholes, which when pieced together in a new configuration generate a new totality.

that are disconnected from their time, scale, size, function and context to produce a new totality. Each floor plan or fragment of a floor plan was first scanned and shared on Archive of Affinities. Operating with a logic of comparison, contiguity and flattened compaction, each plan of multiple fragments is greater than the visible sum.

Making Architecture from Architecture requires that architecture must first be defined and identified. Not everything and anything can be architecture, but what is architecture may at first be unexpected. Making Architecture from Architecture is sympathetic in outlook, so it can discover what architecture is. The approach is relentlessly unbiased, inclusive and opportunistic: no architecture is greater or less than any other. All architecture is equal.

There are three general steps to Making Architecture from Architecture in which Archive of Affinities plays an important role. First is the search, which occurs in a state of controlled randomness. It is not specific nor based on individuals, theories or movements. The material that eventually makes its way into Archive of Affinities is the result of an incremental process of lifting and browsing through old media.

Next is the selection. During the search, architectural images and objects are selected based on their qualities: size, form, shape, mass, proportion, character, posture, figure, organisation, distribution, colour, recognisability and so on. The materials chosen may appear to be wholes, but are to be understood as fragments – extradited from the baggage of their original context and placed into the reserve of Archive of Affinities.

Office Kovacs,
Wedge Gallery installation,
Woodbury University,
Burbank,
California,
2018

The installation aims to realise many of the small models of follies that Office Kovacs produces at a larger scale and size. Elements drawn from the archive are composed together, removed from their prior context and reassembled into a new architectural logic.

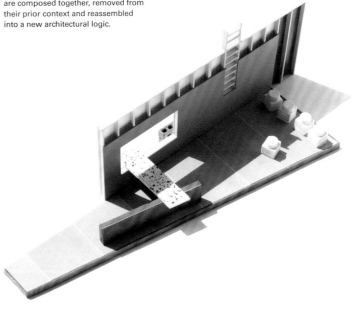

Office Kovacs,
Dog Park,
Los Angeles,
2015

In this masterplan inside a masterplan, each district in the dog park is the result of the repurposed use of objects, either literally or conceptually. The Hypostyle Hydrants district includes a grid of fire hydrants where dogs can relieve themselves. The tops of the hydrants are rigged with sprinklers to clean the area every hour or so.

Office Kovacs,
Archive of Affinities:
Architectural Multiverse,
Graham Foundation for Advanced
Studies in the Fine Arts,
Chicago,
2015

Wall-mounted collage installation made up
of architectural images collected as part of
the Archive of Affinities project. Physical
objects collected for use in the production of
architectural models also formed part of the
collage, displayed in clear bags and placed
next to a ruler as an indication of scale.

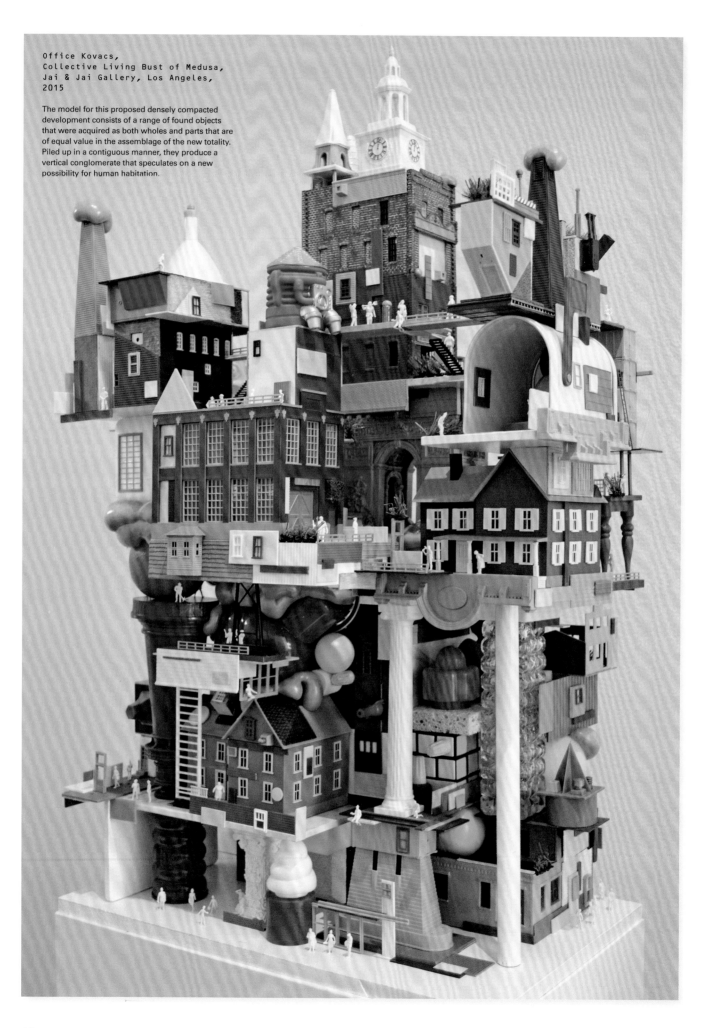

Office Kovacs,
Collective Living Bust of Medusa,
Jai & Jai Gallery, Los Angeles,
2015

The model for this proposed densely compacted
development consists of a range of found objects
that were acquired as both wholes and parts that are
of equal value in the assemblage of the new totality.
Piled up in a contiguous manner, they produce a
vertical conglomerate that speculates on a new
possibility for human habitation.

The final step is the scanning, a levelling device for all gathered images and objects before they are uploaded to Archive of Affinities. The tracked and hunted material is equalised first by scanning and then by archiving. The original context is erased. This record of scanned and archived images is not an end in itself; it is material waiting to be mobilised.

Archive of Affinities is the complete up-to-date digital record of this searching, selection and scanning. It follows a logic of producing affinities. As a continuously growing whole, it reflects personal predilections, tastes and interests, and establishes relationships between digitally recorded images and objects. In the process of its generation, it is a barometer, measuring both individual and collective sensibilities.

Beyond Collection

Archive of Affinities is similar to, but different from, an image bank. An architect's image bank is a way of gathering inspiration and measuring their output with that of the past. At a certain volume of images, the bank inevitably begins to chart lineages between architects and architecture. It conforms to traditional hierarchal structures of time, movements and individuals. Through comparison, it becomes a tool of reference and precedent for architects in their attempts to make architecture from architecture. However, though it is important in this regard, the image bank is limited in

that it has a static existence, trapped by its organisation and file structure, which often results in a convention of disorganisation initiated by file mismanagement, real-time updates and miscellaneous categorisation.

Making Architecture from Architecture operates instead on two levels. The first employs procedures of browsing, searching, tracking, gathering, grouping, organising, comparing, collecting and selecting. The second is the constant production of new images and objects through procedures of flattening, copying, scaling, assembling, combining, compacting, mixing, reorganising, altering, recasting and proposing. What is produced might simply be architectural thought experiments, playful provocations or speculative proposals.

The process takes the material that was tracked and hunted and assembles it. It is ultimately a process of addition. Production is dependent on existing architectural images and objects that have been scanned and recorded in Archive of Affinities. The more that is gathered, the more can be produced. The material that is recorded may exist as a collection within Archive of Affinities, but it does not remain as a collection. A collection is a terminus – once an image or object is acquired it has reached its end. Making Architecture from Architecture employs the logic of a collection, but through Archive of Affinities it ultimately pushes that logic to breaking point. ᴆ

Office Kovacs,
Waterfront Folly,
Toronto,
2017

A proposal for a competition utilising forms and approaches extracted from Archive of Affinities. Composed of a number of walls, it provides a point of relaxation for the citizens of Toronto to observe their surroundings or play hide and seek.

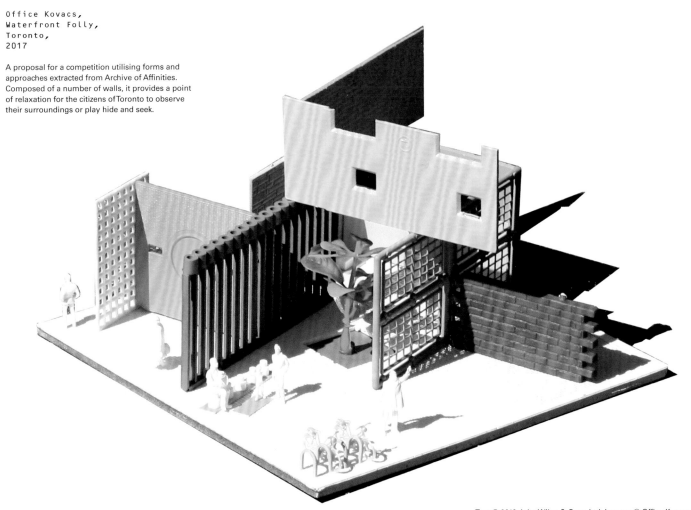

Text © 2019 John Wiley & Sons Ltd. Images © Office Kovacs

Avant-Garde
Legacies

Perry Kulper,
*Speculative House,
Garden + Landscape,
v.83,*
2018

Yellow wandered, promiscuously.
The saturations and hues jumped
a gravity and gathered the
manicured turquoise filigree in
search of ways to live, dream
and revel in the madness of it all.
The uncertain white shadows and
black figures supplied orientation
for the entourage. Drawing in
collaboration with Jeff Halstead.

A Spirited
Flâneur

Perry Kulper

Architect **Perry Kulper**, Associate Professor at the University of Michigan, has produced an extensive set of proto-digital collage-like images inspired by his avant-garde forebears of the 1960s–70s. As he explains, the roots of these visual speculations stretch back a further few decades, to the Dada movement of the early 20th century. All have in common a desire to rethink typologies and transform what is possible.

Perry Kulper,
*Speculative House,
Garden + Landscape,*
v.95, 2018

Nested grains, tweaky resolution, fast and slow surfaces, architecture becoming garden, landscapes, and vice versa. The loss of typological distinction, this time in blues. Drawing in collaboration with Jeff Halstead.

The interests, values and practices of Dada artists anticipated the 1960s–70s avant-garde. Nearly a hundred years ago they constructed avant-garde principles and practices: they are likely responsible for inventing the term and its operations, linked etymologically to the 'advance guard', the 'vanguard' and the 'fore guard'. By grafting nonsense, irrationality and unconventional thinking into the cultural consciousness they produced art that had real teeth. Rejecting reason, their project challenged what was expected. They reconstructed relations between authors and what was produced, upending conceptual, rhetorical and practised habits in art – transforming them, forever. As real cultural renegades they were up to no good. They pulled the rug out from under bourgeois society, and turned their noses up at the aestheticism of a modernist society fuelled by capitalism.

Amongst those who reconditioned ways of making art was the American artist Man Ray. His photographs, particularly *Dust Breeding* (1920), an image of Marcel Duchamp's dust-covered *Large Glass* (1915–23); the rayographs – kinds of quasi or proto-photographs; and his readymades, particularly *Le Cadeau (The Gift)* (1921) – an iron with 13 tacks attached to its sole, all rendered new possibilities for artistic production. The German painter, sculptor and poet Max Ernst's collages, alongside his book *Une semaine de bonté (A Week of Kindness)* (1934) – where he cut up and reorganised Victorian encyclopaedias and novels – triggered alternative techniques for working and constructing significance. Composer Karlheinz Stockhausen rendered controlled chance and indeterminacy in music, opening analogous conversations about predictive and as a result perhaps indeterminate architecture. And notably John Cage, and his experiments with indeterminacy, the development of innovative music scores, his unconventional uses of musical instruments, and his pivotal music composition *4'33"* (1952), flooded the cultural gates. Many of us remain underwater.

Irreversibly, myriad cultural producers have been rerouted by the values, practices and artistic production of the French-American artist and chess player Marcel Duchamp. At a time of need for artistic leadership he hijacked and fuelled nascent and restless imaginations. Around 1913, his framing of 'anti-art' retooled accepted notions about what qualified as art. Equally, he challenged who could make art while opening doors about the cultural agency of conceptual art. His now infamous pseudonym, Rrose Sélavy; his highly varied production captured in *Boîte-en-valise (Box-in-a-Suitcase)* (1935–41) – the portable monograph holding 69 miniature reproductions of his works; and the readymades, reframed the world of everyday objects. Radical work that continues to resonate deeply.

Without question Dada artists were of real artistic and cultural import. Some thirty to forty years later, three 'A's – Florence-based architects Archizoom, London's Archigram and the California-based Ant Farm – took up the architectural and spatial reins, warping what was thought to be possible. Florence's own Superstudio was not in the 'A' category, but demanded attention. The work, writing and performances of these cultural protagonists put lifestyles, institutions and forms of urbanisation at risk, locking avant-garde architectural speculations into the public consciousness. Archizoom's *No-Stop City* (1969–70) argued that advances in technology could reframe the need for a centralised city and bolstered a sense of partial or incomplete architecture and urbanism. In *Walking City* (1964–9), Archigram member Ron Herron visualised large, travelling, technologically motivated and robotically controlled objects that could wander in and around post-apocalyptic urban topographies, shaking the foundations upon which architecture had been built. And Archigram's *Instant City (c 1970)* was Trojan-horse-like in disposition, exploding pop-up-like speculations into tired urban environments. By utilising audiovisual apparatuses, installations and exhibitions transported by large airships they imagined injecting life into dull, monotone urbanisms. My horizon for making drawings and conceiving possible worlds was shifted off-axis when I saw the drawings for this project that utilised the richness of found material to construct possible spatial realms. Superstudio's *Continuous Monument* (1969) was didactic, and successfully upended the disciplines of architecture, urban design and planning. They used easily accessible visual means to elaborate an extreme line of thought about the possibilities of architecture as an instrument for constructing knowledge and agency through visual speculations about total urbanisation. And notably, projects like Ant Farm's *Media Burn* (1975) and *Cadillac Ranch* (1974) added fuel to restless fires.

Domestic Speculations, Digital Collages and Translation
The visual speculations of the design studio Archizoom, the architects Archigram, the architecture, design and media arts-based Ant Farm and the architects Superstudio gave

me room to go out on a limb – many limbs in fact – in the making of 140 collage-like images. Motivated by an interest to learn the 'Quick Selection' tool, these proto-digital images unravel the potential of a few simple Photoshop® operations. Under the rubric of simple programmatic elements – that of domestic, garden and landscape realms – this work rethinks programmatic typologies. By appropriating images – much like the aforementioned practices, but using the Quick Selection tool rather than scissors, to snatch and reassemble some image fragments – a number of interesting things evolved in these very quick visual speculations. An increased range of formal and material possibilities emerged: the generative potential of the history panel – turning layers on and off – offered generative spatial and representational potential; the agency of file sizes, degrees of resolution and scaling opportunities opened things up; and discovering ideas rather than proving them came front and centre.

Speculative House, Garden + Landscape, v.95 and *Speculative House, Garden + Landscape, v.83* are translations of two of the original Photoshop proto-digital collages, here representationally spatialised as they move from the razor-thin flatness of the original images into possible domestic, garden and landscape-like worlds. Like many avant-gardes that challenged what was taken for granted, this work is interested in challenging norms, and opening domestic default assumptions towards probing alternative models for living in relation to natural, synthetic and fictional spatial worlds.

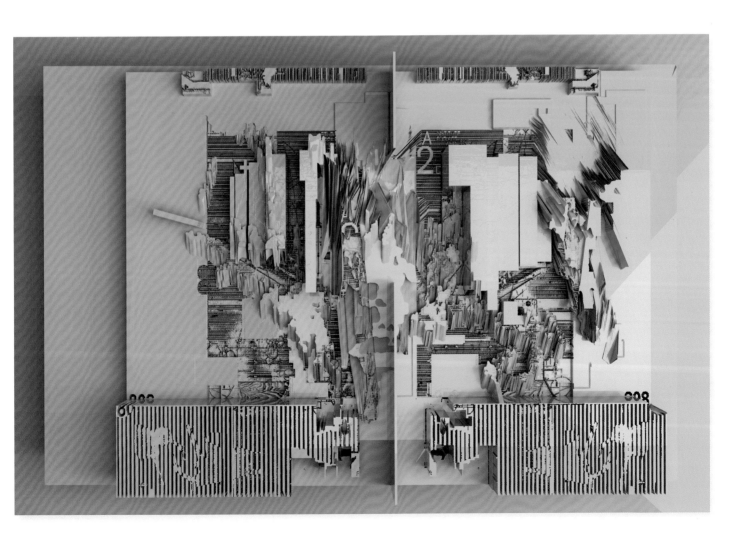

A Current Crop

Over the last 40-plus years, architect and educator Peter Eisenman has framed an understanding of the construction of a discipline, illuminating the discursive positioning of critical thinking, while articulating the value of leveraging deep histories. From 1975 to 2000, John Hejduk guided the Cooper Union School of Architecture, arguably one of the most important architecture education institutions in history, constructing the import of educational frameworks that stand well outside the norm. Additionally, the building of the Southern California Institute of Architecture (SCI-Arc) in 1972 as a critical educational model sits alongside Alvin Boyarsky's retooling of London's Architectural Association from the early 1970s to 1990 – the three schools established a triadic avant-garde of educational legacies, transforming how architects might be educated. And it would be remiss not to touch on the critical import of Robert Venturi and Denise Scott Brown as pivotal role models to many in the discipline of architecture. In his seminal book *Complexity and Contradiction in Architecture* (1966), Venturi's framing of the active use of history, ambiguity as a tactically rich and culturally relevant position, both/and worlds, and the possibility of the difficult whole, continue to serve as transformative road maps for many.[1]

Aerial Acrobats and Sky Writers

Channelling the speculative collages and sometimes irrational projects introduced by the avant-gardes – and from the embers of the world of ambiguity, and both/and, both channelling Venturi – a speculative project arose: three 'Aerial Diptych Follies' that trade on relations of Surrealist-inspired non-human theatricality were concocted. Imagined scenarios and histories, perhaps hundreds of years apart, are enacted by fictional didactic instruments – nonsensical and seemingly purposeless objects, follies as it were, masquerading as aerial acrobats. Collectively they propagate myriad combinations of paired worlds into plausible but indecipherable wholes. They crack open the imaginative potential of the object-instruments and the events to which they refer and that they might falsely (re)construct.

Perry Kulper,
*Aerial Diptych Folly,
v.01: Hello World,*
2018

Living in the hidden spaces of the quantifiable harvesters, everything from light to landscape is disguised as a signifier of itself. Only the avatar sits proudly, because, well … he is a toad. Drawing in collaboration with Oliver Popadich.

Collectively they propagate myriad combinations of paired worlds into plausible but indecipherable wholes.

Perry Kulper,
Aerial Diptych Folly,
v.03: Frontal,
2018

Innocuous blue suddenly spawns
portals to a virtual audience – a place
over there, absent of anything other
than material likenesses. Drawing in
collaboration with Oliver Popadich.

Perry Kulper,
Aerial Diptych Folly,
v.02: Oculus,
2018

In a place where shadows can light
the ground, trace nothing at all, or
simply cease to exist, what then is
light? Drawing in collaboration with
Oliver Popadich.

In the development of this work *Aerial Diptych Folly,
v.01: Hello World*; *Aerial Diptych Folly, v.02: Oculus*; and
Aerial Diptych Folly, v.03: Frontal attempt to get under the
metaphorical digital hood, chasing what might be possible
by interrogating conversations between image-making and
digital-modelling practices. Interestingly, the manual practices
of drawing and compositing cut-up material in the original
'Aerial Diptych Folly' analogical drawings, in the manner of
some of the avant-gardes, has given way to a now more
ubiquitous domain of keyboard operations – in a sense
trivialising the act of making and perhaps eliminating latent
knowledge construction acquired in that act while gaining
speed and the potential of diverse appropriated materials.

Continuing to probe the digital realm, the key motivations
for this work are linked to augmenting default positions
frequently practised in the space of digital modelling –
including the nuanced interplay of 3D modelling towards the
production of 2D images, and vice versa. A number of things
were discovered in the process of pursuing these modelling
translations: shadow and light become highly configurable
in render space and are key in their manipulation of 2D
imagery; light sources negate shading and shadow effects,
thus appearing as flat objects, enabling their transformation
into notational markings that affect the geometry of the
composition; shadows can be turned off, or altogether
transformed, collapsing space, confusing relationships or
producing novel effects (such as shadowed lighting); texture
mapping and image mapping can obfuscate or redefine our
understanding of the 2D image or 3D space; and finally, given
that these effects play out a single privileged viewpoint,
utilising the three-dimensionality of the model allows the
creation of new 2D imagery that redefines a layered spatiality,
masked entirely by the original view.

With other freedoms granted by avant-garde artists and architects the *Floating Bird Motel, v.03: Sky Writer* utilises collage-thinking, programmatically, reframing the familiar human-centric programme of a motel. Tactics deployed are linked to utilising loaded programmatic elements – a float/shrine, a theatre, an honorific bird or talisman, dispersed houses and house fragments, the construction of an artificial-weather-systems garden, and a translation of Marc-Antoine Laugier's primitive hut (1755).[2] In combination with a site undergoing constant construction and reconstruction as evidenced by a log, this hypothetical project reroutes human–non-human relationships, deploying various technologies, programmes and material formations to rethink human dominance over other life forms.

Floating Bird Motel, v.03: Sky Writer – Artificial Weather Garden, Sky Writing and a Working Log; *Laugier's Hut*; and *A Float'ish Shrine* are kinds of digital model/image-making composites, enabling heterogeneous ideas to co-mingle in search of a synthetic but indeterminate whole. Interests in the project include: the development of non-perspectival space; mixing natural and machine technologies; articulating artificial and real temporalities; and thinking about multiple aerial lifestyles. Ultimately, by challenging norms, and by varying the material, atmospheric and situational conditions of the motel, this project establishes a sense of familiar strangeness through the juxtaposition of distant realities in this floating motel'ish proposal for birds.

Perry Kulper,
Floating Bird Motel,
v.03: Sky Writer –
Artificial Weather
Garden,
Sky Writing and a
Working Log,
2018

Bottled trade winds construct navigational horizons, tracing comings and goings. Autumn lightning harvests, winter white-outs, 'hailing' spring(s) trumpet the release of wet, aerial stuff, with a dash of sonic ambience. Summer-breezed balloons parade about while sky-writing bubble wands draw a gifted entourage. Drawing in collaboration with Karl Heckman.

Under the Skin

Cumulatively, avant-garde thinking and production has opened a great deal in my thinking and production. I know I do not stand alone in this regard. Cultural agents of many kinds have been given conceptual freedom, enabling imaginations to travel promiscuously – releasing gravity, material realities, durations and timeframes into new statuses, combinations and hybrid formations. These latitudes have released known epistemological models and categories into the wild, rebirthing what might be possible.

The avant-gardes played big. They moved conceptual terrains, challenged construction logics, scalar relations and the agencies of representation through a real politics of communication. They rerouted educational and practised grounds by envisioning social, political, infrastructural and technologically promiscuous environments that shook established grounds, real and conceptual. They were children of the 1960s that helped to configure pop culture, challenging what was taken for granted. All the while they rendered possible worlds through the drawings, writing and performances they offered. The production of collages, combinatory worlds of possibility that were constructed from found material, in particular, changed what was possible.

Implicitly and explicitly my efforts have traversed the precedents set by many avant-gardes. Many have utilised their game-changing insights and production techniques, aspiring to the spirit, the tone and intensity for which their work laid the ground, reframing what is taken for granted and augmenting what is expected. They were big game changers, to say the least. They sent depth charges through a complacent world, transforming it forever. ∆

Perry Kulper,
Floating Bird Motel,
v.03: Sky Writer – Laugier's Hut,
2018

opposite: Primitive, maybe. They retreated, and colonised it, mixing technologies, constructing mini-sky drawings. Emerging onlookers lurked nearby – aerial acrobats all. Drawing in collaboration with Karl Heckman.

Notes
1. Robert Venturi, *Complexity and Contradiction in Architecture*, Museum of Modern Art (New York), 1966.
2. Marc-Antoine Laugier, *Essay on Architecture* [*Essai sur l'architecture*, 1755], translated by Wolfgang Herrmann and Anni Herrmann, Hennessy & Ingalls (Los Angeles, CA), 2009.

Perry Kulper,
Floating Bird Motel,
v.03: Sky Writer –
a Float'ish Shrine,
Domestic Passengers
and a Logged Sidecar,
2018

With feathers in their caps they came from far and wide, they were all good eggs – snow birds, birds of a feather, a bird in the hand, and free birds, all. Partridges, pear trees, you name it. They were up with the lark, dreaming of 13 ways of looking at a blackbird. Drawing in collaboration with Karl Heckman.

Text © 2019 John Wiley & Sons Ltd.
Images © Perry Kulper

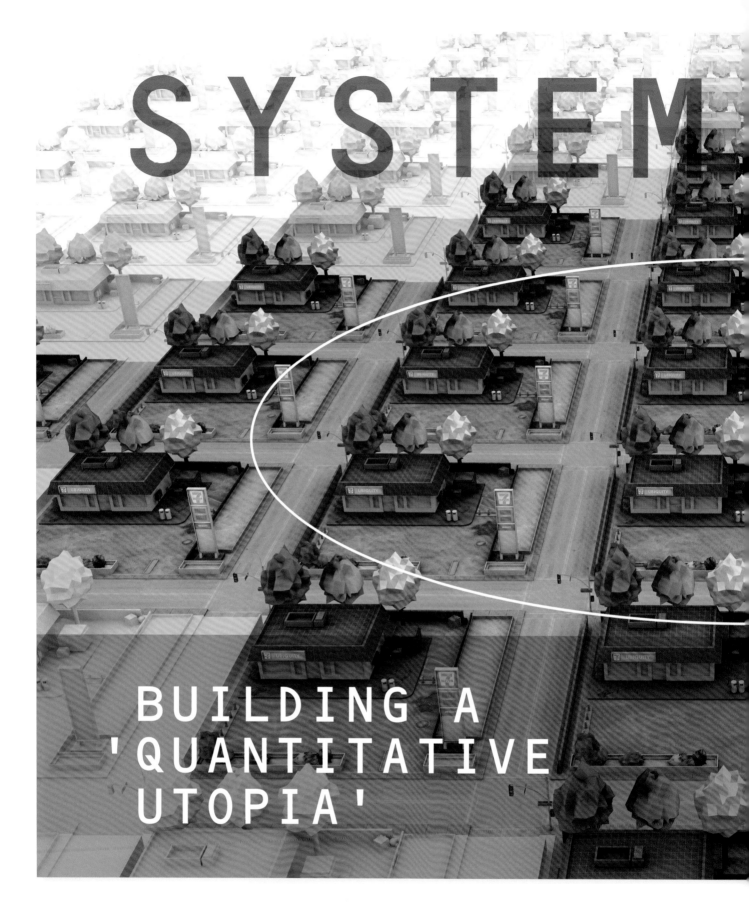

SYSTEM

BUILDING A 'QUANTITATIVE UTOPIA'

Luke Caspar Pearson,
Ubiquity digital game, 2016

This screenshot drawing of the game
demonstrates an infinitely repeating landscape
of 'superarchitettura': generic supermarket
buildings that grow around the eye of the
player and follow his or her movements.

CITIES

There is a connection between theoretical schemes such as Archizoom's *No-Stop City* and the virtual and augmented worlds of today. Guest-Editor **Luke Caspar Pearson**, Director of the Undergraduate Architecture Programme at the Bartlett School of Architecture, University College London, explores video-game spaces and his own architectural gaming environments, demonstrating their resonance with avant-garde concepts.

Luke Caspar Pearson

The projects of radical architects working in the 1960s and 1970s had a resounding effect on architecture by redefining the discipline and cutting through Modernism's relationship to technology. These conceptual projects – 'negative utopias'[1] such as Archizoom's *No-Stop City* (1969–70) – presaged architecture's current obsessions with digital data and information systems. Branzi said as much, positing that utopia was only now possible through 'quantitative' means.[2] Marie-Ange Brayer argues that Branzi, along with the rest of his collaborators in the Italian Radical group Archizoom, developed positions where 'the city was now a concept, a "behavioural model," and no longer a place'.[3] Yet what we cannot forget is that many of the concepts and models emerging at this time were allied to subversive thoughts and an emphasis on civic playfulness and leisure.

Archizoom were not alone in this respect. Fellow Italian Radicals such as Superstudio and UFO were designing hippyish collages, mobile systems and reconfigurable cities alongside wearable structures and nightclubs. Ettore Sottsass developed a collection of trippy drawings explaining a post-work society that probed the depths of human pleasure in *The Planet as Festival* (1972). Elsewhere, Yona Friedman, Archigram and Cedric Price had all proposed infrastructural projects that could accommodate the mores of playful users. Constant Niewenhuys's *New Babylon*, begun in the 1950s, represented an architecture where 'there is only the playful drifting' of *homo ludens* (man at play) 'through an infinite and endlessly manipulable interior space'.[4] *Homo ludens* was of course the title of Dutch historian Johan Huizinga's seminal 1938 work on play and games that is still much referenced today.[5] Some of Archizoom's famous mirrored-box models for *No-Stop City* were built using the same Pepper's Ghost techniques used in arcade games of the day (such as the 1972 Dune Buggy by Midway), allowing them to express their repetitive landscape through a prototypical form of virtual space.

These radical architects foregrounded the relationship between concept and cutting-edge technology, society and leisure. Their methods pose interesting questions for contemporary digital discourse in architecture focused on the utility of computation in fabrication, machine learning or parametric technologies. Although *No-Stop City* programmatically predicted the quantitative world of the automated Amazon warehouse or the numerically controlled assembly line, in fact what the project itself – as an unrealised utopia – may have truly foreseen is the rise of virtual spaces, the world of video games and virtual reality. Here technology allows for the parallel existence of worlds that allow us to partake in fictions, synthesise new identities and hold a mirror up to society in a similar manner to these historical projects. Most virtual worlds are entertainment media and regarded by many as folly, yet their structure and particular forms of kitsch reinvigorate ideas of what a quantitative utopia could be as an echo of the conceptual spaces originally produced by the avant-garde.

From Utopia to Atopia

The megastructures and 'negative utopias' of the 1960s and 1970s were never realised. They existed on paper or in models, and their organisational systems were mainly

metaphorical yet often inherently playful and game-like. As games theorist Jesper Juul argues, all game structures require a form of 'immaterial support',[6] a mutually agreed establishment of certain rules that are not physically manifest. In Archizoom's world, these invisible rules were the flows of information that structured the city and allowed for new, unlimited possibilities within the isotropic grid. This ties closely to French philosopher Louis Marin's definition of utopia as 'the product of a process by which a specific system is ... changed into another system with its own coordinates, structures, and grammatical rules'.[7] If this manipulation of elements within an infinite grid was the quantitative utopia Branzi had spoken of, such utopias exist almost everywhere today in all manner of navigable virtual worlds. The popular building game Minecraft (2009), which has become a form of ersatz architectural design software, uses a voxel-based structure that is an isotropic system where each block in the world requires another block to attach itself to. Visually and ontologically, a three-dimensional grid system structures the world, a form of immaterial support defining the operations of the playful world within. Minecraft is a visually striking example of this, but isotropic grids are ubiquitous to nearly all modern 3D design software used to create architecture and virtual environments. Relationships between objects in virtual worlds (in games or in CAD) are always defined in relationship to their Cartesian position, orientation and movement. If Archizoom's 'Superarchitettura' (1966) was informational 'super-consumerism, of the supermarket, superman, and super-petrol',[8] then today we could add Super Mario to this list.

Archizoom,
No-Stop City: Residential Parking,
1970

Archizoom's mirrored boxes created prototypical virtual spaces using Pepper's Ghost techniques, and cabinetry that recalled arcade games of the period, blurring the lines between architecture and media, play and concept.

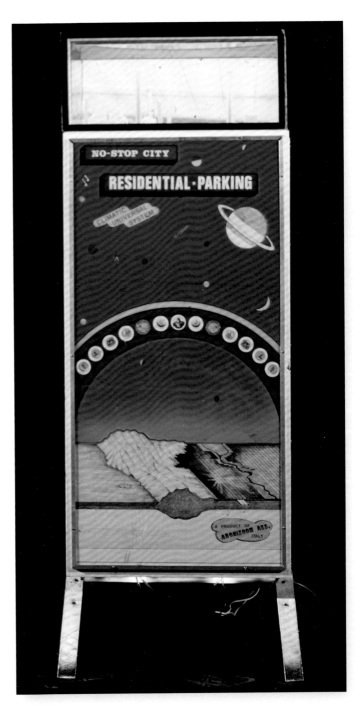

Archizoom,
No-Stop City,
1969–70

Peering into mirrored boxes, viewers could see a virtual space unfold in front of their eyes. Through optical reflection the quantitative utopia could emerge as a repetitive infrastructure of information to be appropriated by citizens.

Most virtual worlds are entertainment media and regarded by many as folly, yet their structure and particular forms of kitsch reinvigorate ideas of what a quantitative utopia could be

Interestingly, research conducted by Rowland Atkinson and Paul Willis found that supermarkets portrayed in game worlds are spaces where players blend the virtual with reality in a condition they call the 'ludodrome'.[9] The proliferation of branding and graphic iconography, along with quantitative spatial organisations makes the supermarket a space that is just as banal in the virtual or the real and therefore becomes a portal between the two. Not only has Superarchitettura become the prevailing logic of our physical world, but it also serves as a syntactic junction between the real and the virtual.

Super-Ubiquity

The connection between paper projects and virtual spaces brings utopian thought into the present. McKenzie Wark describes virtual game spaces as 'atopian', which is the quantitative utopia by any other name. Wark argues that 'if Utopia thrives as an architecture of qualitative description, and brackets off quantitative relation, atopia renders all descriptions arbitrary. All that matters is the quantitative relations.'[10] In this context, Superarchitettura inspired the video-game-based project Ubiquity (2016), which replicates the landscape of generic signs and symbols contained within the modern supermarket into a game world that unfolds and spreads around the movements of a player within an isotropic grid. In Ubiquity, Superarchitettura is explored at several scales. The player moves from an urban realm of generic minimarts to an infinite landscape of shelves filled with processed products. After some time wandering through this repetitive landscape, the player can enter a box of cereal and mingle among the grains within. Here we see a negative utopia of super-consumerism at the micro scale, blobs of toasted rice-and-sugar paste forming an architectural landscape of super-manufactured foodstuffs.

Luke Caspar Pearson,
Ubiquity digital game,
2016

A drawing showing the player's journey from the generic architecture of the supermarket to the air-conditioned environments of innumerable shopping aisles and ultimately into the world of super-processed foods.

Archizoom,
No-Stop City,
1969–70

Within their mirrored-box environments, Archizoom suggested virtual zones where citizens could pitch tents and build encampments in between the ephemera of super-consumerism. Such spaces could be constantly rearranged within an infinite grid.

In Ubiquity, the virtual world and its extents are defined at an informational level like *No-Stop City*'s mirrored infinities, but through computational code rather than optics. As the player moves, the game code builds and destroys objects upon a grid dynamically based on the view extents of a virtual camera. Switching to an isometric viewpoint, the player can see the landscape of minimarts unfolding around them from above, as these extents are defined in real time by the perspective camera of the main first-person view. The movement of the player-character expands the isotropic system as it goes, establishing a feedback loop that shapes the world itself. Yet the invisible isotropic grid is always there, providing a datum point as architecture is assembled in real time. As Brayer argues, Archizoom established a project where architecture was 'an environment that was constantly being reshaped, inscribed in the moment',[11] which could almost serve as a dictionary definition of how the virtual game world – or indeed any other – works. This can be evidenced when attempting to understand their logics through drawings and other cartographic practices, for example in the research project Noclip World (2016), which peers beyond the edges of game spaces. In such an environment, any disruption to this constant inscription can cause atopia to build up into a distorted landscape, a city lost in an abundance of informatic signals.

In such an environment, any disruption to this constant inscription can cause atopia to build up into a distorted landscape, a city lost in an abundance of informatic signals

Luke Caspar Pearson,
Noclip World,
2016

As part of a research project examining virtual environments, the drawing explores the invisible forces and rules that act on architecture experienced within a game world and how they structure the experience of that world.

Rules Versus Representation

Of course, an atopia growing around a singular player is solipsistic. Similarly, Archizoom's mirrored box assembles an isotropic world only when viewed. However, computational developments have meant that in virtual worlds, systems can now self-produce quantitative utopias. Techniques known as 'procedural generation' are used by game developers to produce worlds through algorithms. This typically involves the design of architectural components – not dissimilar to Superstudio's histograms– which are then composed through a programmed system. The world generated is entirely quantitative, but also possesses the qualities of the original components placed into the system. This recalls Yona Friedman's prototypical Flatwriter (1967), an early form of design software for users to create their own living spaces within his *Spatial City* (1958), but fictional worlds of games often take this further. The game No Man's Sky (Hello Games, 2016) autonomously creates a whole universe from scratch, with each planet different for every player. Game developers Big Robot also developed a system called The British Countryside Generator (2014) for constructing a virtual world based on the rolling hills of the UK as a procedural parochialism, a romantic fantasy of a picturesque landscape created with advanced computation.

Another game designer, Strangethink, develops procedural worlds, for example Secret Habitat (2014), which produces a series of buildings containing a network of art galleries. Every piece of art within the galleries (and its title) is also generated through the algorithm. Here, the quantitative utopia is taken to its ultimate extent with the system-driven creation and dissemination of human culture, all born from the same algorithm as the architecture that houses it. This negative utopia deals with the contemporary world of images: their creation and dissemination, which has been radically changed by computer systems. Such techniques are often conceptual and ironic in their definition of spatial relationships. A procedural world is formed through the connection between the symbolic component objects and the system governing their placement. Such a relationship between playfulness of experience and a systemic playfulness of meaning was of course explored by Archizoom at the object scale in their furniture series for Poltronova (1967), where beds and chairs became satirical, ironic objects that conveyed messages about consumerism through the context in which they could be placed.

In response, the game-based project DWG Hunter (2017) also uses procedural generation to explore these informational relations in which the player must find and repair deviations while jumping on revision clouds. The world is assembled through architectural units that are automatically attached to one another at designated junctions alongside layers of random objects assembled upon a grid, defining an isotropic world that is arbitrary and yet carefully cultivated. By pressing a button, the player can reassemble a new world around them. Here, multiple different quantitative utopias reside within one program. Each discrete unit of architecture is defined through its relationship to the next, but each of them also possesses a symbolic position. A grid of tiled plazas is generated, upon which monumental entrances lead to bridges that go nowhere or towers that hover in the air.

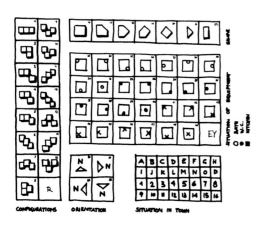

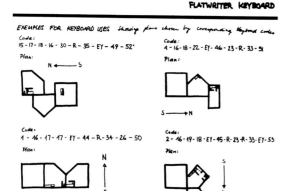

Yona Friedman,
Flatwriter,
1967

Friedman's work on adaptable structures extended to the design of this computer program, which allowed users to design their own living spaces as a precursor both to CAD software and virtual spaces.

Strangethink,
Secret Habitat digital game,
2014

Screenshot from the game showing a virtual gallery space procedurally generated by an algorithm, housing artworks and names also produced by the same computational system.

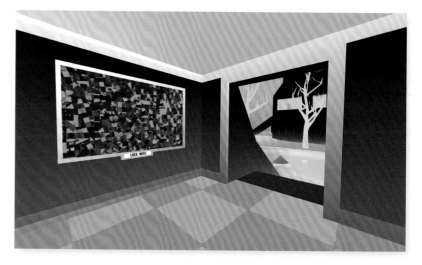

Luke Caspar Pearson,
DWG Hunter digital game,
2017

One of the compositional outputs produced by a procedural system. Various symbolic built components are arranged through a computational system that can be manipulated by the player to create infinite variations.

Screenshot composition drawing of the architectural spaces generated by the procedural system. Spatial tropes are combined and exploded at will through the actions of the player who can reshape their atopia around them.

All these architectural paradoxes are, like Archizoom's utopic projects, the result of the rational pushed to its tipping point. The irrepressible march of the frame-by-frame computer code creates a utopian space only to be overwritten the moment the player interjects once more. The system only cares about connections and quantitative relations even if the architectural elements resemble something like John Hejduk's or Aldo Rossi's architectural characters assembled human-centipede-style into a snaking conga line. The game space becomes a form of random monument generator where architectural tropes become combined together over and over in the isotropic realm. In this respect, the virtual architecture seeks to question the relationship between history, symbolism and computational systems. The real-time computation of the game engine can be used to assemble architecture quantitatively through algorithms while the qualitative properties of that architecture carries relations to historical forms and typology. As a conceptual space it enmeshes avant-garde influences with the atopian structure of our contemporary (virtual) worlds.

Game Space as System City

The system cities of the architectural avant-garde were conceptual spaces that questioned the logics of capitalist reality and the discipline of architecture itself. Computational technologies have allowed for all manner of quantitative utopia and atopia to be realised, most of which do not carry the subversive charge of the radicals. But this does not mean that they could not. By inviting people into isotropic domains and foregrounding relationships between systems, virtual environments are both an extension of the critical world-building projects of the avant-garde, and a new medium by which avant-garde architectural practices can be reinvigorated and re-imagined. We will build new system cities, where computation meets concept, rules meet representation and interface meets ideology. Here we can come to terms with architecture in our information age through building new negative utopias, moving from the factory towards the hyper-connected threads of virtual and theoretical worlds. ⌂

Notes
1. Pino Brugellis and Manuel Orazi, 'Radicals Forever', *Radical Utopias*, Quodlibet Habitat (Rome), 2017, p 38.
2. Andrea Branzi, *No-Stop City: Archizoom Associati*, HYX (Orléans), 2006, pp 176–9.
3. Marie-Ange Brayer, 'The Radical Architecture Project as "Territorial Design"', *Radical Utopias*, Quodlibet Habitat (Rome), 2017, p 50.
4. Mark Wigley, *Constant's New Babylon: The Hyper-Architecture of Desire*, Witte de With Center for Contemporary Art/010 (Rotterdam), 1998, p 13.
5. Johan Huizinga, *Homo Ludens: A Study of the Play-Element in Culture*, Routledge (London), 2003.
6. Jesper Juul, *Half-Real: Video Games between Real Rules and Fictional Worlds*, MIT Press (Cambridge, MA and London), 2005; Kindle edition for iPad, Loc 526.
7. Louis Marin, *Utopics: The Semiological Play of Textual Spaces*, Humanities Press (Atlantic Highlands, NJ), 1984, p 242.
8. Text from exhibition poster for Andrea Branzi et al, 'Superarchitettura', Galleria Jolly 2, Pistoia, Italy, 1966.
9. Rowland Atkinson and Paul Willis, 'Charting the Ludodrome', *Information, Communication & Society*, 10 (6), 2007, p 818.
10. McKenzie Wark, *Gamer Theory*, Harvard University Press (Cambridge, MA and London), 2007, note 119.
11. Marie-Ange Brayer, *op cit*.

Text © 2019 John Wiley & Sons Ltd. Images © Images: pp 70-1, 74(t), 75, 77 © Luke Caspar Pearson; pp 72, 74(b) Courtesy Studio Andrea Branzi; p 73 © Andrea Branzi/CSAC-Università degli Studi di Parma; p 76(l) Yona Friedman, Fonds de Dotation Denise et Yona Friedman, all rights reserved. Photography Jean-Baptiste Decavèle; p 76(r) © Strangethink Software

Jimenez Lai

THE FUNCTION OF UTOPIA

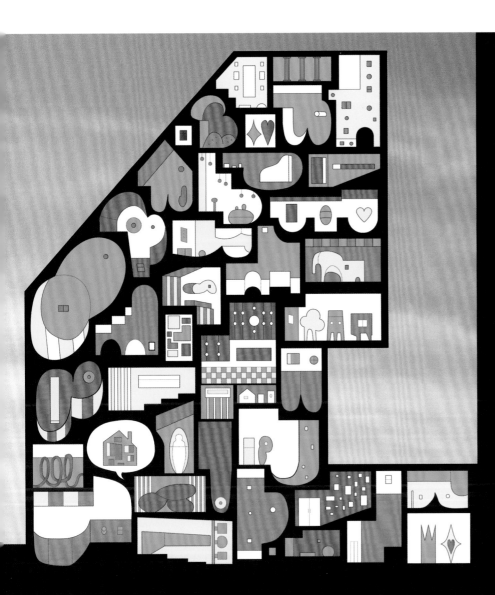

Jimenez Lai/Bureau Spectacular,
Cartoonish Metropolis,
2012

The project imagines a series of buildings
looking and existing as a kind of comic
strip, with each individual dwelling as a
separate narrative. The drawing style takes
cartoonish curve-types as elements of an
architectural section.

What is a utopia's function other than as a platform
upon which we reflect the reality we already live in?
Jimenez Lai, founder of Los Angeles studio Bureau
Spectacular, argues that in facilitating criticism,
utopias can point the way to solutions for current or
future challenges. Drawing parallels between utopian
visions in literature and the cartoon caricatures of
modern journalism, he presents a series of utopic
graphic novels that he has produced which explore
issues from hyper density to zero gravity.

Jimenez Lai,
Babel,
2009

Published as part of the graphic
novel *Citizens of No Place*
(Princeton Architectural Press,
2012), *Babel* tells the story of a
12-kilometre (7.5-mile) tall tower
taking the footprint of Central Park
in Manhattan.

As a vehicle to reveal contemporary issues, speculative projects of architecture and urbanism often re-tell stories about the worlds that the authors identify with. In doing so, these utopian projects provide a lens through which an audience can look afresh at their own worlds. 'Utopia', in its etymology, does not describe an 'ideal place'. Rather, utopia is a 'no-place' (from the Greek *ou-topos*). Utopia is an alternative world, a clean slate – a space that allows for commentaries to exist, turning architecture into a critical project.

In Thomas More's book *Utopia* (1516), a fictional island was used as a parallel universe to be a space of satire. By suspending conditions of reality, More was able to produce a commentary on the status of the monastery from a written work of hyperbole. Utopia, in this sense, occupies a space not so dissimilar to the political commentary editorials or newspaper cartoon caricatures within the field of journalism. Not all utopias are built the same way: depending on the time, space and cultural zeitgeist, different concerns will play out in different ways. Utopia is the no-place that allows critical projects to be written.

The problems of post-1968 Italy were very different from those of 16th-century England. Superstudio, alongside Archizoom, dealt with very specific Florentine issues in their own ways. The impending collapse of Late Modernism was coinciding with other significant concerns. These architects had experienced a lifetime of mass-produced consumerism and understood its implications. Secondly, the status of architectural education in Italy had become self-contradictory. Florence was a ground for preservation rather than construction, meaning architecture and education became Sisyphean acts of inaction upon inaction. Finally, the 1966 flood of the Arno became a point replacing a city with a no-place. Realising that architecture may not be solely about buildings, or even the preservation of buildings, the exhibition 'Superarchitettura', held that year at Galleria Jolly in nearby Pistoia, began a process of meta-criticisms by works of 'design'. Utopia, or a suspension of disbelief, suddenly became Superstudio's *Continuous Monument* (1969) and Archizoom's *No-Stop City* (1969–70). These spaces of hyper-examination were also spaces of meditation: it is only in an impossible world that architects can construct scenarios in which we have the time and space to re-examine who we are.

As they demonstrated, utopia is not just a no-place – it is a journalistic, editorial instrument for architects. Through their representational expertise, architects can construct plausible worlds to re-imagine our own. But what is the role of parodies, parables, satires or caricatures? In the retelling of the realities we live in, acts of journalism through architecture and urbanism are never unbiased. Yet, it also seems critical that we fully understand the power that utopias wield as a journalism through the describing of worlds.

Architectural Education as a No-Place

The education of an architect is a strange one. The design studio is a constant state of make-believe: a mostly fictional proposition is placed upon a real or fictional site, delivering some notion of contemporary solutions. There is no true examination period the way that lawyers or doctors write exams. In their place, architects perform soliloquies. The verbal performance of an architect uses models and drawings as a puppet theatre that they are evaluated on. Following Thomas More, we might ask: Do architects require fiction to fully exercise themselves? Is it productive for architects to learn how to master the acts of persuasion via performances of utopias? Such performances can allow something rationally outlandish to become an irresistible sensorial project.

In Harry G Frankfurt's essay *On Bullshit* (1986), he examines the relationship between lying and bullshitting.[1] Lying, an undertaking while aware of the presence of truth, is a deliberate act to cover something up. Bullshit does not require the presence of truth. In the spirit of 'fake it till you make it', bullshitting is a bluff that has the potential to be taken so far that it might become real. In the context of architecture studios, the relationship between 'fake' and 'real' oscillates delicately where factual sites and fictional projects are discussed with equal scales of investment. Architectural education, as an endeavour that celebrates a blank slate upon which one imagines wildly and imaginatively, constantly refreshes a journalistic examination of our society every semester. It requires tabula rasa to be both rational and sensorial. But this can be positive: the utopic can compel people to maintain their scepticisms, doubts and curiosity to question existing power structures.

Jimenez Lai,
Future Archaeologist,
2009

Future Archaeologist is another excerpt from *Citizens of No Place*. It is a story about an archaeologist 10,000 years from now, investigating the evidence left behind by humans at the beginning of the 21st century; evidence that exists predominantly as endless fields of suburbia.

Citizens of No Place

The year 2008 was a turbulent time economically for many people, but particularly for young architects. During that time, I worked on a series of utopic graphic novels that reflected upon the many situations I lived in. Economic constraints had prevented built work from being the primary pursuit for most young architects, so I primarily focused on what some characterise as 'paper architecture'. These speculative imaginings of no-place were an apt instrument within academic environments, allowing many thought experiments to be explored rapidly.

In 2012, *Citizens of No Place* was published by Princeton Architectural Press, with a grant from the Graham Foundation.[2] The book is a graphic novel comprising 10 chapters set within the same universe. From spaceships travelling at the speed of light, to towers scraping the bottom of the stratosphere – each story asked questions about the status of architecture upon a tabula rasa. These were questions about the status of 'formalism', secessionism and political conservatism; unfixed orientations of orthographic projections from the lack of gravity; the status of suburbanism, the urban conditions of extremely tall buildings or the plight of future archaeologists discovering our world today. *Citizens of No Place* was not only a speculative project, but an editorial on the world retold through the means of utopic architecture and urbanism.

that's great! next question..

Jimenez Lai/Bureau Spectacular,
Tower of Twelve Stories,
Coachella, California, 2016

below: Tower of Twelve Stories was a 16-metre (52-foot) tall structure at the 2016 Coachella Valley Music and Art Festival in California. The structure represents a fictional tower block whose form is influenced by elements seen in comic books.

Scenario-Building: Speculative Utopias and Utopic Meta-Narratives

Within *Citizens of No Place*, there are a few typologies of cartoons. There are speculative utopias and utopic meta-criticisms. *Future Archaeologist* was a story about the status of 'this' (academic work) versus 'that' (constructed edifice). Reflecting Victor Hugo's notion of 'this will kill that ... the book will destroy the building',[3] cartoons became a platform to re-examine the reality of the early 21st century. During a road trip from Wisconsin to Arizona in 2004, I noticed that the education of architecture had little to no impact upon the built environment in the United States. Most residential architecture can be built without the participation of architects. Whether 'Victorian', 'Spanish' or 'Modern' in style, this landscape is filled with cookie-cutter houses. My narrative speculates that future archaeological digs will yield an overwhelming body of evidence of our cultural monotony. It also explores the mismatch between documents of architectural academia and the architectural edifice in the field. The meta-criticism here is to highlight the growing gap between the insular nature of autonomous conversations within the 'discipline' of architecture versus the actual constructed edifices.

However, speculative utopias create quite a different typology of storytelling. They create hyperbolic conditions based on existing circumstances in the world. In extreme scenarios, architecture becomes a whole world within which there are physics, economics and sociopolitical realities to be regarded. *Babel*, for example, is a 12-kilometre (7.5-mile) tall tower constructed atop the footprint of Central Park in Manhattan. Peaking around the troposphere, it can accommodate over 80 million humans – roughly the size of Germany. Within this tower, there are jurisdictions and political zones responding to cloud conditions – a sectional urbanism. The function of such a utopia is to take hyper density seriously as a condition and examine the architectural and urban qualities within it. It was because of the *Babel* experiments that I was able to later propose extreme sectional conditions like the *Cartoonish Metropolis* (2012), which was translated to our project Tower of Twelve Stories (2016) for the Coachella Valley Music and Art Festival in California.

Similarly, *Noah's Ark, In Space* (2005) was a vehicle to think about the programmatic ramifications of zero gravity. Without gravity, the interior of architecture becomes an unfolded continuous surface – every plan, section or reflected ceiling plan becomes a surface programmable for human action. Seeing surface in such a way made projects like the *Phalanstery Module* (2008) or *Continuous Landscape* (2017) conceivable.

Jimenez Lai,
Noah's Ark,
In Space,
2005

opposite: Also published in *Citizens of No Place* is *Noah's Ark, In Space* – a story about a phalanstery, a city inside of a building. The city is a Noah's Ark fleeing Earth, a city without gravity.

Jimenez Lai/
Bureau Spectacular,
Phalanstery Module,
Los Angeles,
California,
2008

left: *Phalanstery Module* is an installation that rotates once an hour, allowing a surface to become parallel to the ground every 15 minutes, as well as a perfect 45-degree oblique every 7.5 minutes.

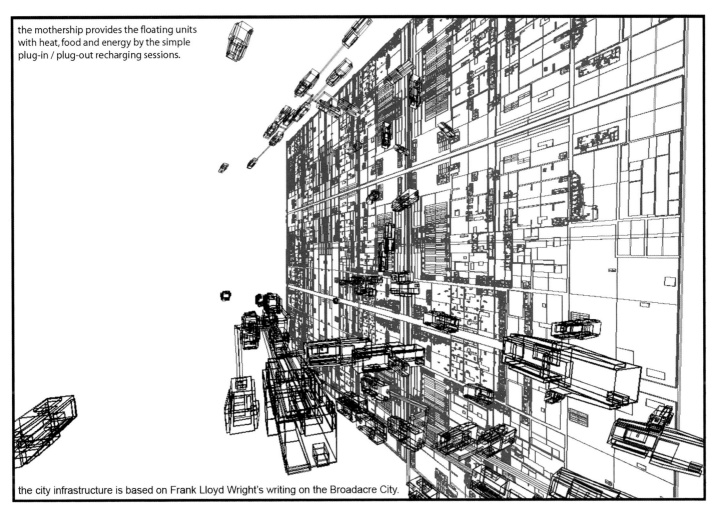

the mothership provides the floating units with heat, food and energy by the simple plug-in / plug-out recharging sessions.

the city infrastructure is based on Frank Lloyd Wright's writing on the Broadacre City.

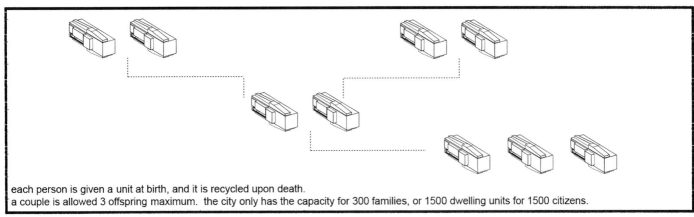

each person is given a unit at birth, and it is recycled upon death.
a couple is allowed 3 offspring maximum. the city only has the capacity for 300 families, or 1500 dwelling units for 1500 citizens.

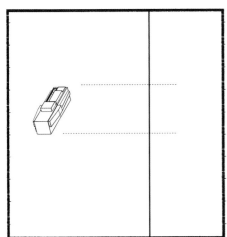

(guys farming moss for photosynthesis.)

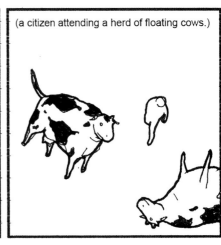

(a citizen attending a herd of floating cows.)

Sensibility Building: Cartoonish Architecture

Projects like Archizoom's *No-Stop City* allowed them to develop their sensibility as designers in the impossible platform that is utopia. However, the American tradition of paper architecture is slightly different from the utopian meditations of Italy and England. For Daniel Libeskind or Bernard Tschumi, speculative drawings became the signature from which architectural sensibilities were created. Even Ant Farm's *House of the Century* (1973) contained design decisions where the compositional choices came from the paper studies. Such an approach was also key to the work of John Hejduk and Peter Eisenman. In the contemporary American academic world this remains largely the same – many of today's 'paper architects' work primarily on the honing of sensibilities rather than constructing scenarios. As a utopian project, *Citizens of No Place* allowed me to address both.

Beyond my scenarios, two stories (not in the book) – *When I Grow Up* and *Sociopaths* (both 2013) – explicitly developed architectural sensibilities. These stories used speech bubbles and cartoon frames to weave sensibility studies into and out of the narrative. In *Sociopaths*, the 'Rashomon effect' of inconsistent testimony allowed three separate houses to be described by three witness accounts of the same event. This not only allowed me to examine historical references like the *Raumplan* planning method of Austrian architect Adolf Loos (1870–1933), but also enabled new design experiments to emerge. In 2014, I entered a hiatus on telling linear stories – after drawing *Inside Outside Between Beyond*. Instead, cartoonish architecture became a sensibility to be explored. Scenario-building requires cartoons to be about architecture, thus making 'cartoon' the medium and 'architecture' the subject matter. In contrast, cartoonish architecture refocuses 'architecture' as the medium and 'cartoon' as the sensibility.

In Sociopaths, the 'Rashomon effect' of inconsistent testimony allowed three separate houses to be described by three witness accounts of the same event

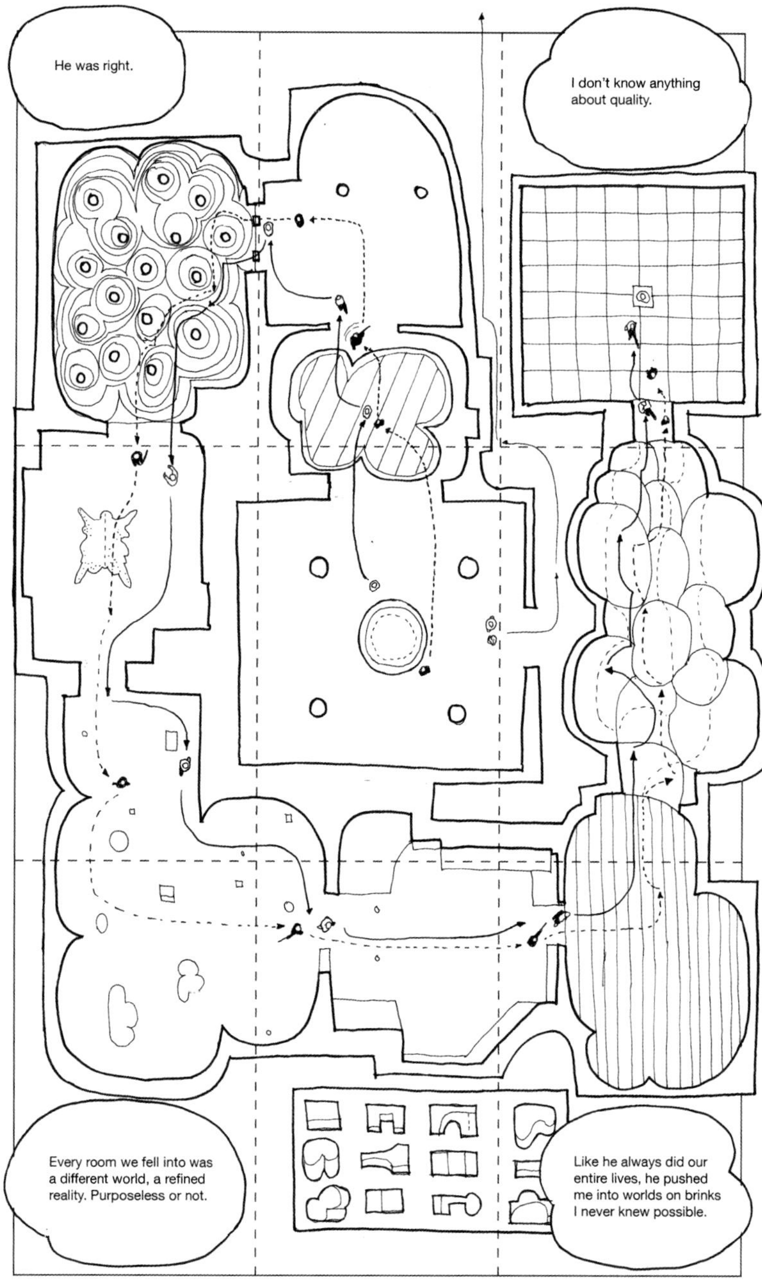

Jimenez Lai,
Sociopaths,
2013

Sociopaths is a story about the murder of a billionaire. It tells of three witnesses, all suspects, each with conflicting testimonials, describing a completely different house within which the murder takes place.

Jimenez Lai,
When I Grow Up,
2013

When I Grow Up is a story about three graduating kindergarteners imagining the types of futures they will have when they grow up. They imagine what houses they might live in, which workplaces they might work in, and ultimately what environments they will live in in the future.

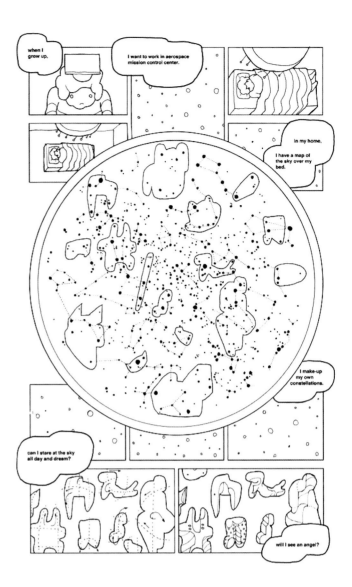

Parafictions and Hyperrealities

In the last decade, the notion of 'fact' has been in a strange place. With world leaders labelling unfavourable journalism 'fake', or news sources being unable to remain 'objective', the contemporary media cycles leave a nauseating maelstrom of words that cannot be trusted. In her 2009 essay 'Make Believe: Parafiction and Plausibility', art historian Carrie Lambert-Beatty examines a genre of work that plays on the overlap between fact and fiction.[4] We might think of actor and comedian Sacha Baron Cohen's exaggerated fictional characters who reveal the true tendencies of those he talks to. For example, Baron Cohen disguised himself as an Israeli ex-military gun advocate called Erran Morad to infiltrate conversations about gun control in the US. His performance was so plausible it convinced 'real' people like gun-rights activist Philip Van Cleave and former US Vice-President Dick Cheney to take his mask as a matter of fact. The coexistence of fact and fiction becomes a work of journalism of hyperbolic caricaturisation of both the fake and the real. This links closely to philosopher Jean Baudrillard's notion of hyperreality, where consciousness is unable to distinguish between reality and a simulation of reality.[5] The representation of utopia in architecture and urbanism is not so dissimilar to such parafictions and hyperrealities. Architects, through their arsenal of representational skills, can produce notions of realities without constructing them. These realities, place or no-place, are critical to re-examining our world. If the generations of the 1960s and 1970s channelled their anxieties into the utopias we now know well, oncoming generations of architects should also use their expertise to tell us new stories about their worlds. ⌀

Notes
1. Harry G Frankfurt, 'On Bullshit', *Raritan Quarterly Review*, 6 (2), 1986, republished as a separate volume by Princeton University Press (Princeton, NJ) in 2005.
2. Jimenez Lai, *Citizens of No Place*, Princeton Architectural Press (New York), 2012.
3. As stated by Archdeacon Claude Frollo in Victor Hugo's novel *The Hunchback of Notre Dame* [*Notre-Dame de Paris*] (1831), book 5, chapter 1.
4. Carrie Lambert-Beatty, 'Make Believe: Parafiction and Plausibility', *October 129*, Summer 2009, pp 51–84: www.mitpressjournals.org/doi/pdf/10.1162/octo.2009.129.1.51.
5. See, for example, Richard G Smith and David B Clarke (eds), *Jean Baudrillard: From Hyperreality to Disappearance – Uncollected Interviews*, Edinburgh University Press (Edinburgh), 2015.

Text © 2019 John Wiley & Sons Ltd. Images: pp 78–80, 81(t), 82–5 © Jimenez Lai; p 81(b) © Jimenez Lai, photo Jeff Frost

These realities, place or no-place, are critical to re-examining our world

FEVERISH DELIRIUM

SURREALISM, DECONSTRUCTION AND NUMINOUS PRESENCES

Through his current drawing work, *D*'s Editor **Neil Spiller** traces the protagonists of MoMA's 1988 'Deconstructivist Architecture' exhibition back to the Surrealists and their engagement with Paris as a great engine of chance, liberating the coiled-up and unseen properties of objects.

Neil Spiller,
Longhouse: Exterior of the Chicken Computer,
Glade of the Chicken Computer,
Communicating Vessels,
2008

The striped tent that houses the Chicken Computer is perched
above a pool reminiscent of Giorgio de Chirico's *Mysterious Baths*
(1934–8). The image is laden with Surrealist references, particularly
from De Chirico's oeuvre.

**Imagine the perplexity of a man outside
time and space, who has lost his watch,
his measuring rod and his tuning fork.**

—Alfred Jarry, *Exploits and Opinions of
Doctor Faustroll, Pataphysician*, 1898–9[1]

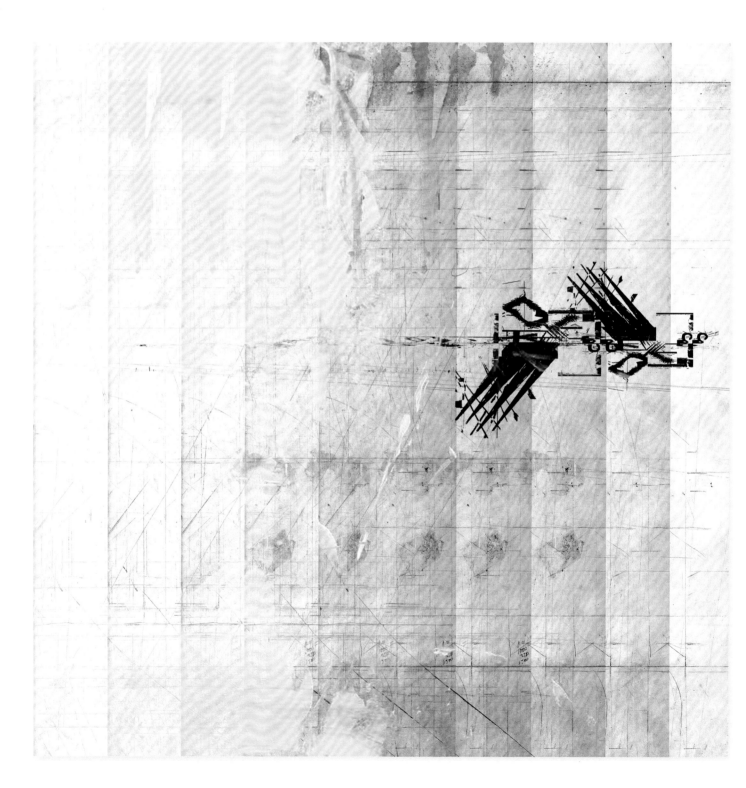

[The] city's inhabitants create an exquisitely complex geometry, a geography passing beyond the natural to become metaphysical, only describable in terms of music or abstract physics; nothing else makes sense of relationships between roads, rails, waterways, subways, sewers, tunnels, bridges, viaducts, aqueducts, cables, between every possible kind of intersection.

—Michael Moorcock, *Mother London*, 1988[2]

In the catalogue for the 1988 'Deconstructivist Architecture' exhibition at the Museum of Modern Art (MoMA) in New York, architectural theorist and historian Mark Wigley declares that the architects exhibited (Zaha Hadid, Frank Gehry, Bernard Tschumi, Daniel Libeskind, Coop Himmelb(l)au, Rem Koolhaas and Peter Eisenman) are not utopian avant-gardists due to their (in his eyes) engagement with building and the notion of the contemporary city. Rather, Deconstructivism 'attempts to get under the skin of a living tradition, irritating this from within. Deconstructivist architecture locates the frontiers, the limits of architecture, coiled up within everyday forms. It finds new territory within old objects.'[3]

This trying 'to get under the skin' of the everyday has always intrigued me, particularly with the wealth of new technologies currently afforded to us as architects and designers. It is often suggested that my work is 'utopian', but it is not. There is no attempt to create visions of utopic architecture. It seeks instead to explore the potentialities of new technologies on architectural space and form, but to do so outside of the rather limited, well-trodden furrows of other contemporaries by using drawing and writing as scrying devices to try to see into the future – good or bad.

The intention of this article is to claim Deconstructivist architecture, so powerful an influence on me as a student and young architect in the 1980s, for the Surrealist cause – an artistic conjunction illustrated here by a useful series of spatial protocols and tactics in my most recent work – the *Longhouse*. The centrepiece of my 20-year Communicating Vessels project, the *Longhouse* (started in 2015) deals with mythology, mnemonics, augmented reality and surreal numinous presences. It determines its own augmented-reality spatial arrangements and characters in conversation with a virtual deconstructed doppelgänger that scans the varied spatial and artistic contexts within which it is constantly cast.

Neil Spiller,
The Longhouse in Repose,
Communicating Vessels,
2018

The house without its virtual
and augmented components,
as figured ground.

The City Under Siege

Art historian Roger Cardinal, in his seminal essay 'Soluble City' in the 1978 issue of *∆* dedicated to *Surrealism and Architecture*, defined the six Surrealist readings of the city/landscape as a dream, as a love affair, as a palimpsest, as a poetic text, as a psychic labyrinth, and as a system of signs[4] – readings that are simultaneous and concurrent and certainly find new territories with old objects. The flea market, the municipal park, the arcade and the simple perambulation through the streets in search of intoxication, desire and love provide the engines that power this maelstrom of objects and vectors.

Likewise, Wigley describes Deconstructivism as having the same creative imperative of making objects where materials become exotic as sudden bomb blasts of strangeness, and each project draws out 'previously unnoticed disruptive properties … making them thematic. Each thereby assumes an uncanny presence, alien to the context from which it derives, strange yet familiar – a kind of sleeping monster which awakens in the midst of the everyday.'[5]

The similarities between the Surrealist way of seeing objects and the city, and the Deconstructivist one, as described by Wigley, comes as no surprise. Many of the architects featured in the MoMA exhibition had previously drunk from the marvellous well of Surrealism during the 1970s: Bernard Tschumi with his event spaces, which were inspired by French dramatist and poet Antonin Artaud (1886–1948) and literary figure and philosopher Georges Bataille (1897–1962), explored through the geometries of his *Manhattan Transcripts* (1976–81) and further elucidated in his *Parc de la Villette* scheme for Paris (1982–98); Rem Koolhaas and his *Delirious New York* Surrealist odyssey, published in 1978; and the automatic sketching of Co-op Himmelb(l)au, akin to the automatic writing of the Surrealists, which encouraged pure written streams of consciousness – to name a few examples. But perhaps the most imbued in Surrealist mythology and indeed the most recognisable Deconstructivist is Daniel Libeskind.

Inspired by the Surrealists and proto-Surrealists like Alfred Jarry, Libeskind's theoretical works such as *Micromegas* (1979) and *Chamber Works* (1983) are highly complex drawings that oscillate between architecture, notation and vectors. Still, a few clues to his inspirations are left for us to decipher within this cacophony of finely executed lines, boundaries and prisms reminiscent of Italian draftsman,

Neil Spiller,
*A Mannequin Form Starts to
Appear in the Longhouse,
Communicating Vessels,*
2018

The house mixes all manner of ideas and forms based on what its doppelgänger virtual self is sensing, conditioned by the mysterious and random Chicken Computer.

Giovanni Battista Piranesi's unbuildable fantasy Carceri (1750). For example, in one of the *Micromegas* drawings, *Maldoror's Equation*, is that an umbrella we see within it?[6] The latter work is a clear reference to the French poet Comte de Lautréamont and his work *Les Chants de Maldoror* (1868–9) from which the Surrealists adopted his expression of desiring beauty as the 'Chance Meeting on a Dissecting Table of a Sewing Machine and an Umbrella'.[7]

Libeskind's *City Edge* (1987) project for Berlin, exhibited at the MoMA 'Deconstructivist' exhibition, is an audacious work that shares its genealogy with *Micromegas* and *Chamber Works*. It is full of Surrealist enigma, equivalence of objects, a palimpsest revealed, a graphic poetic text and indeed a psychic labyrinth – a place where strangeness abounds yet highly contextual to its urban position. It is a Surrealist hybrid, a tumultuous maelstrom writ large across its site, a cacophony of vectors, multiscaled material parts and spatial striations. The archetypal city as described by Moorcock above, yet pimped to the level of a contagion; a dream or a nightmare presided over by an inclined beam-like infernal engine. Things are not what they seem; liberties are taken with the protocols of architectural modelling and drawing – nothing utopic here.

Ferocious Images of Desire

In 1972 the British novelist Angela Carter, channelling Surrealism, published *The Infernal Desire Machines of Doctor Hoffman*, quoting at its beginning Jarry's sentence above. Like Libeskind's *City Edge*, Carter's book is set in a

landscape of strangeness. The narrative conforms to Cardinal's definition of the six aspects of Surrealist landscape; nothing is what it seems, time and space are disrupted and nonlinear. As Ali Smith writes in the introduction to the 2010 edition, it 'takes apart the "machines" of love, of narrative, of social structure in a fusion (and simultaneous analysis) of fantasy, *fin de siècle* richness, pastiche, sci-fi thriller, postmodernism, picaresque, quest literature, adventure story, pornography and political and social theorizing'.[8] Its protagonist Desiderio has likewise lost his tools with which to calibrate the world as he makes his haphazard way through a series of urban and rural landscapes full of Surrealist visions, cataclysmic events and pornographic detours powered by his foe's (Doctor Hoffman) desiring machines. These machines, driven by copulating couples, are responsible for the unravelling of space-time, the confusion between dream and reality, and the creation of a menagerie of numinous chimeric inhabitants and mises-en-scène that populate the novel.

Some of my favourite scenes in Carter's book are when Desiderio discovers a peepshow proprietor in a striped tent, on a pier reminiscent of Southwold's in the UK, filled with seven viewing machines, each bearing an enigmatic phrase. In 'The Eternal Vistas of Love' machine, for example, two eyes stare back at the hapless voyeur. Many of the machines' contents are allegorical, pornographic and murderous, and unbeknown to Desiderio predict crucial scenes in his journey to find Doctor Hoffman and kill him to restore order to the city. There are shades of Marcel Duchamp's *Étant donnés* (1946–66), his last artwork, where one looks through two eyeholes in a door to view a mysterious scene simultaneously pornographic, mythic and maybe murderous. The striped tent also invites thoughts of Giorgio de Chirico's *Mysterious Baths* (1934–8) series of paintings and drawings and the built sculptures of them in Milan. Other resonances include Aldo Rossi's *Cabina* (1981).

Later in Carter's novel we find out that the peepshow proprietor was Hoffman's teacher at university and is keeper of his 'museum', a sack of small boxes containing models, slides and pictures used to change the scenes within the peep machines: 'men, women, beasts, drawing rooms, auto-da-fes … He held out a bouquet of ferocious images of desire in my direction … "the symbols serve as patterns or templates from which physical objects and real events may be evolved."'[9]

Disembodied Spectres

Like Libeskind's *City Edge*, Carter's terrains are beyond simple codification and symbolically multivalent. Thirty or more years on from *City Edge* and more than 45 since Carter's novel, technology has evolved and the digital revolution has created many spatial opportunities not open to the Surrealists and Deconstructivists. As Smith writes of Carter's novel: '[This] imaginistically cornucopic and virtuoso performance is a visionary book for the virtual age.'[10]

Today's spacescapes are a rich mix of the virtual and the actual. The complex clusters of architectural elements and interactions that exist within the Communicating Vessels project are a network of ascalar, reflexive inputs and outputs; some actions impact on actual geographies, and some on

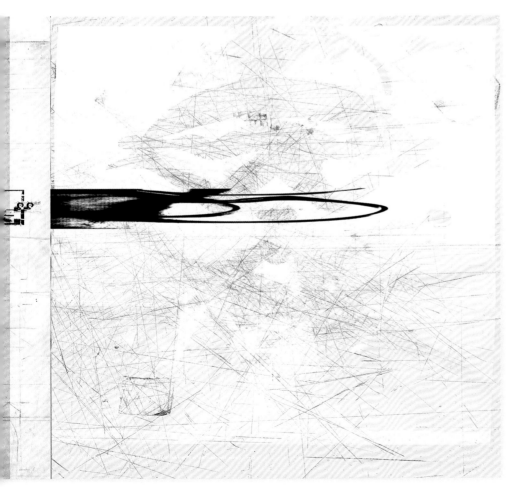

Neil Spiller,
Longhouse: Trajectories of the 'Hearts and Parts' Figure,
Communicating Vessels,
2018

The *Longhouse* plan and the vectors of the augmented-reality mannequin at a certain point, illustrating this numinous presence's form.

virtual geographies, and this relationship continues to change as the spaces remix themselves due to chance occurrences. There are no rules, dogmas or doctrines in these spaces, which will have their own rarefied spatial logics. Nothing is too surreal, too hyperlinked nor too hybridised. Nothing is spatially verboten and nothing is impossible, architecturally speaking, any more.

The *Longhouse* is inhabited not just by the real Professor who lives in it accompanied by his dreams, desires, memories and inventions, but also by a series of augmented-reality numinous presences. Some are based on mythic characters – a Minotaur (so beloved by the Surrealists and name to one of their journals), Hermes, Hecate, Iris and angels – but others are inspired by Surrealist works: a boxing match in a virtual vitrine, mannequins, nudes descending staircases and Baconesque forms. The augmented-reality, strange geometries of the house add many dimensions to it, their trajectories and appearance uncontrolled by the inhabitant

Neil Spiller,
Longhouse: The Progress of the Mannequin I,
Communicating Vessels,
2017

The numinous presence of an augmented-reality mannequin emerges from outside the Longhouse, through its wall, and is seen within.

as the house defines them in a parallel virtual world defined by the pecks of chickens within the mysterious Chicken Computer, itself within a red-striped tent. This system of chance choreography in effect does what Wigley describes Deconstructivist architecture as doing, but with 21st-century technology: 'The geometry proves to be much more convoluted: the sense of being enclosed, whether by a building or a room, is disrupted … rather, the wall is tormented – split and folded. It no longer provides security by dividing the familiar from the unfamiliar, inside from out. The whole condition of enclosure breaks down.'[11]

Neil Spiller,
Longhouse: The Progress of the Mannequin II,
Communicating Vessels,
2018

The presence of the mannequin here becomes more defined, and
as it moves, the space around it more disturbed and gothic.

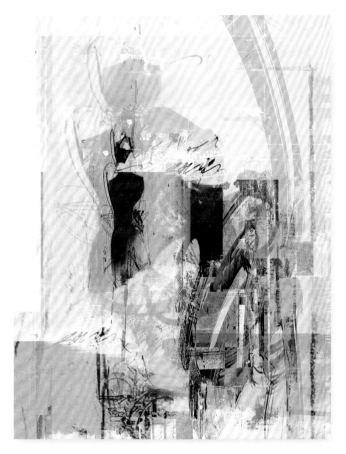

From a Surrealist point of view, the breakdown of the enclosure – in the case of the *Longhouse* the domestic enclosure – was investigated early on. Max Ernst produced his collage novel *Une semaine de bonté* (*A Week of Kindness*) in 1934.[12] It is a series of collages challenging the domestic interior of the time, a haven of erotic and oneiric images populated by chimeric beings, strange weathers, violence and shame. At one point in her novel, Carter takes Desiderio and the Count (a character half-Dracula and half-Marquis de Sade) to a brothel inside which features the Bestial Room of hybrid animal and furniture fitments and inhuman prostitutes consisting of unlikely sexual paraphernalia. Like Ernst's collages, this room is 'a refuge for those who can find no equilibrium between inside and outside, between mind and body or body and soul, vice versa, etcetera, etcetera, etcetera'.[13]

The inhabitant of the *Longhouse*, a Professor of Surrealism in the age of augmented reality, has sought to re-create this choreography of Surrealist surprise within the house. Augmented-reality presences pass through it, reminding him of his past, of his possible futures, and providing astounding juxtapositions of ideas and forms as a way to dislocate his creative self, to develop his inventive thoughts beyond the logical or established. Of course, the Professor can choose not to see these presences, but when he does this they still go about their business in the unseen dimensions of virtual space. The drawings of these spaces show all simultaneously in a specific time perhaps never to be repeated. The *Longhouse*, therefore, comes from a genealogy of displacement, disjunction, rupture, event and the twisting of architectural space as per the Deconstructivists, and the Surrealists before them – a key series of tactics used repeatedly by the avant-garde. ⅅ

Notes
1. Alfred Jarry, *Exploits and Opinions of Doctor Faustroll, Pataphysician* (1898–9), in *Three Early Novels: Collected Works II*, ed Alastair Brotchie and Paul Edwards, Atlas Press (London), 2006, p 210.
2. Michael Moorcock, *Mother London*, Secker & Warburg (London), 1988, p 7.
3. Philip Johnson and Mark Wigley, *Deconstructivist Architecture*, Museum of Modern Art (New York), 1988, p 18.
4. Roger Cardinal, 'The Soluble City: The Surrealist Perception of Paris', ⅅ *Surrealism and Architecture*, 48 (2–3), 1978, pp 143–9.
5. Johnson and Wigley, *op cit*.
6. Neil Spiller, *Architecture and Surrealism: A Blistering Romance*, Thames & Hudson (London), 2016, p 203.
7. Comte de Lautréamont, *Maldoror and Poems*, Penguin (New York), 1988, pp 216–17.
8. Ali Smith, 'Introduction', in Angela Carter, *The Infernal Desire Machines of Doctor Hoffman* [1972], Penguin (London), 2010, p viii.
9. *Ibid*, pp 110–11.
10. Smith, *op cit*.
11. Johnson and Wigley, *op cit*.
12. Max Ernst, *Une semaine de bonté*, Éditions Jeanne Bucher (Paris), 1934.
13. Carter, *op cit*, p 156.

Neil Spiller,
Longhouse: The Progress of the Mannequin III,
Communicating Vessels,
2018

The mannequin fades, becoming less defined, and the spatial field
around it becomes less distorted, migraine like, as it disappears.

Text © 2019 John Wiley & Sons Ltd. Images © Neil Spiller

Sarah Dunn and Martin Felsen

Behind
the Wheel

UrbanLab, Filter Island, Chicago, 2014–15

Natural sewage-treatment processes take place in a series
of large bioremediation 'bowls'. As water flows through the
island from one bowl to the next via small streams, it becomes
successively free from harmful substances. Filtered water is
then safely released into Lake Michigan.

Charles Darwin
and Superstudio
Do the Driving

Sarah Dunn and Martin Felsen, partners in Chicago-based practice UrbanLab, are inspired by the Japanese Metabolists, Charles Darwin's work on Ascension Island and the legacy of Superstudio. Their aim is to reinvigorate Superstudio's notion of positing alternative models of life on earth. Using this concept, they have been able to design urban landscapes that utilise the same flexible evolutionary strategies for a modern, digital and ecologically sensitive world. Here they illustrate their design imperatives with two projects, Filter Island in Chicago and Re-Encampment in Death Valley, California.

It takes time to build a utopia. Luckily, some designers are patient and are willing to stand by while their ideal creations slowly evolve and come to fruition. For example, in 1836 Charles Darwin began a process of transforming Ascension Island – located over 1,000 miles (1,600 kilometres) from Africa and South America – from a waterless volcanic desert into a tropical rainforest. When he first landed on the island it was a British military base to which food and water were delivered from a distance. Darwin devised a plan to also ship in plants and trees in order to transform Ascension's ecology from desert to garden.[1] His plants and trees took root on the island's highest peak, and captured clouds to stimulate precipitation. In turn, rain saturated the volcanic soil, which created favourable conditions for further plantings to grow and thrive. Over time – several decades – the thick, newly planted fields and forests became a self-sustaining and self-reproducing ecosystem, bearing provisions like water, food and habitat. Today, the island remains a remote oasis in the middle of the Atlantic Ocean.

Darwin planned and executed the conditions for Ascension Island to evolve into a higher form of existence; that is, he provided it with internal agency, not a 'masterplan' dependent on externally imposed decision-making. In contrast to Ascension Island, in the 1960s the Aral Sea was the world's fourth-largest lake, linking Uzbekistan and Kazakhstan, then the states of the Soviet Union. Today, it is a desert. Prior to the 1960s, the Syr Darya and Amu Darya rivers supplied the Aral Sea with water. But, in an attempt to grow food in the surrounding desert, Soviet leaders devised a masterplan for diverting the two rivers. Without incoming water, the lake slowly disappeared. Over-exploiting the Aral Sea's ecosystem rather than preserving or even strengthening it has caused chronic economic paralysis for the surrounding populations. In addition, today, salt, fertilisers and chemicals from crops continue to seep into the exposed lake bed, imperilling its long-term health and vitality.

At the Aral Sea, bureaucratic decision-making and masterplanning caused irreparable harm. On Ascension Island, Darwin revitalised a barren desert by redesigning its topography to mimic a self-organising natural system. Darwin steered the island to evolve organically without the need for external guidance.

From Ascension to Filter Island

Several of UrbanLab's projects attempt to revisit concepts from architects – especially mid-20th-century modern architects – who, like Darwin, sought to utilise long-term design strategies that favour continual change rather than one-time masterplanning. Filter Island (2014–15) reclaims some of the design approaches Kenzo Tange adopted in the 1960s to leverage intractable problems and invent new urban forms that could slowly emerge and evolve over time. His large-scale Metabolist projects speculated on how city-scaled megastructures could influence an architecture-based urbanism to address current and predicted urban challenges, coupling resilience with sensitivity to identity and place.

Both Filter Island and Tange's Toyko Bay (1960) project attempt to steer urban growth to accommodate the

Public amenities increase or decrease in frequency based on their positioning on the Filter Island. Public programmes are sparse near the mouth of the river where inflowing water begins the treatment process, and densest where water is clean and safe, illuminating the purification process for the public.

Each of the ecological/cultural bowls is bounded by corridors of trees and grasses – fuzzy or defined upper edges, or 'rims' – that provide permanent, dry passageways through the island. These outer edges cause or prevent permeability and cross-fertilisation between the various bowl ecologies.

movement of people, pollution and natural resources. In both cases, bodies of water – Lake Michigan and Tokyo Bay – are regarded as vital resources that require long-term planning and preservation. They are designed to broker exchanges between long-lasting public infrastructure including parks and mobility corridors, and smaller, ever-changing programmes such as cultural venues and housing. However, Filter Island does double duty: in addition to providing a sustainable method of naturally cleaning drinking water for millions of people, the project also proposes a new recreational amenity for the city. Today, Chicago's source for clean drinking water, Lake Michigan, is periodically contaminated by sewage during heavy rain storms. Filter Island intercepts and de-toxifies this sewage before it has a chance to enter the lake. Ecological services overlap with cultural amenities: public programmes including stadiums and theatres, beaches and sports fields, and gardens and biodiversity reserves are interwoven with water-purifying bowls. Taking cues from Darwin, both Filter Island and Tange's Toyko Bay project speculate on driving the future of cities by specifying componentry that will undergo natural development (however artificial at the outset) by increasing in size and changing physically with maturity.

The goal of replacing planned cities with the grid was to enable equality and opportunity

Counter-Utopian Plans and Actions

Paralleling Tange and the Japanese Metabolists, in the 1960s several other groups were trying to envision and steer the future of the planet, most notably Superstudio. Instead of using traditional utopian design strategies that responded to suboptimal circumstances with favourable alternative projections, Superstudio developed countercultural manifestos steeped in science fiction and big data. In *Life: Supersurface* (1972), a network – or physical grid – that people could tap into to access energy and communication-enabling systems, was the group's response to the earth's (ongoing) deterioration, with rueful provocations depicting prescient yet pragmatic counter-realities.[2] The goal of replacing planned cities with the grid was to enable equality and opportunity. As Superstudio wrote in 1972, 'by the elimination of the city, we mean the elimination of the accumulation of formal structures of power in search of a new free egalitarian state in which everyone can reach for different grades in the development of his possibilities, beginning from equal starting points'.[3]

UrbanLab,
Re-Encampment,
Death Valley,
California,
2015-17

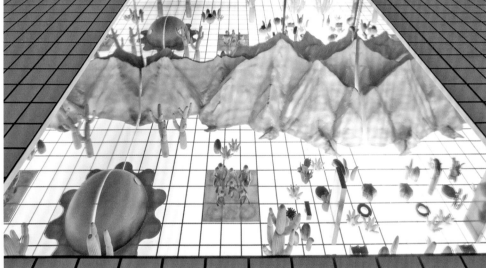

Model re-creating a Superstudio counter-design postulation on how to steer the earth towards a new highly connected utopian plane composed of only the most essential life-supporting elements of air, heat, water, food and telecommunications.

An endless environment divested of all but a few essential elements, the model re-examines, as did Superstudio, the essence of architecture within the connected landscape.

The Re-Encampment aqueduct is a structure of practical and cultural exchange, its 'main street' promenade a long, thin plaza that stretches across the arid landscape. Mixing infrastructure and architecture has a long history – the 'Old' London Bridge (completed 1209) and the Ponte Vecchio (1565) in Florence, for example.

The aqueduct here takes on a different urban form – a new town made up of courtyard voids and programmed solids, aggregated around the public space of the promenade.

UrbanLab's Re-Encampment project (2015–17) is a homage to Superstudio, and an attempt to continue the conversation of the group in their explorations of 'alternative models for life on earth'.[4] Superstudio's psychedelic collages coax a future-oriented inventory of architectural effects out of benign environments, void of traditional architectural constructions. Re-Encampment re-enacts artificial panoramas and sublime landscapes to provoke a collective imagination suggesting a future free from 'repetitive work', which Superstudio saw 'as an alienating activity'.[5] The original *Supersurface* grid was a deliberate aesthetic that involuntarily blended nature and infrastructure in ways that are familiar to us today. This dichotomy goes beyond the world of physical objects to highlight the tangle of invisible networks vital to our livelihood and to our potential freedom.

Working on similar themes in the 1960s, US film director Stanley Kubrick also envisioned the means of influencing planetary evolution. In his *2001: A Space Odyssey* (1968), a mysterious form of artificial intelligence – embodied as black monoliths – observes planetary progress and nudges inhabitants' behaviours when shifts in evolution are deemed necessary. Not unlike Darwin, who set in motion the long-term transformation of Ascension Island, Kubrick pictured a process ultimately aiming for purposeful outcomes. Neither utopia was masterplanned, but rather created through processes of incremental, local inputs reciprocally affecting a state of continual change. UrbanLab's Re-Encampment also explores the physical extrusion of Kubrick's monolith and the thickening of Superstudio's grid into a singular yet multifunctional form: an aqueduct. For centuries, aqueducts have symbolised our technological ability to harness nature and domesticate the landscape. For Superstudio, this type of technological/architectural hybrid epitomises a preferable, benign environment: looking up one sees sky; looking down one sees a continuous infrastructural surface to tap into, anywhere. Like the eco-social infrastructure of Filter Island, Re-Encampment, in Death Valley, California, sustains life, this time in a harsh desert environment. As the aqueduct, as both infrastructure and architecture, passes through the valley it takes on different forms of urban encampment. ⌀

Notes

1. Charles Darwin, *The Voyage of the Beagle*, vol 29, PF Collier (New York), 1909, p 494.
2. Superstudio, 'Life: Supersurface', *Casabella*, 367, 1972, pp 15–26.
3. Emilio Ambasz. 'Italy: The New Domestic Landscape', press release, Museum of Modern Art, New York, 1972, p 5: www.moma.org/momaorg/shared/pdfs/docs/press_archives/4824/releases/MOMA_1972_0053_46X.pdf.
4. *Ibid*, p 2.
5. *Ibid*. p 5.

Connecting miles of public programme – sometimes sparse, sometimes dense – here the aqueduct is a mini-city, with neighbourhood-like patches of form that fit together above and below the promenade.

Text © 2019 John Wiley & Sons Ltd. Images: pp 94-7, 99 © UrbanLab; p 98 © Michelle Litvin Studio

PLAY IT

IN CONVERSATION WITH

PLAY IT

PLAY IT

ARCHITECT SAM JACOB

PLAY IT

PLAY IT

PLAY IT

AGAIN
AGAIN
AGAIN

Matthew Butcher *&* Luke Caspar Pearson

AND ARTIST PABLO BRONSTEIN

AGAIN
AGAIN

AGAIN

Architecture and art are symbiotic disciplines. Architect **Sam Jacob** and artist **Pablo Bronstein** use tactics of performance, role play and enactment to both provoke and understand their individual practices. Robert Venturi and Aldo Rossi loom large as key influences in their expansive propositions. Guest-Editors **Matthew Butcher and Luke Caspar Pearson** met with them in Bronstein's East London studio to discuss the meaning behind their use of historical architectural references within the development of their work.

Artist Pablo Bronstein and architect Sam Jacob have both forged significant careers around the creation of mimetic relationships to historical architectures and architectural styles. Utilising ideas and practices associated with performance and re-enactment, they have developed work with close links to the concepts of architects operating in the 1960s and 1970s including Robert Venturi and Aldo Rossi. By recontextualising the methods of these figures in a 21st-century setting and challenging existing disciplinary hegemonies, Bronstein and Jacob have created a particular aesthetic position focused on the pleasures and possibilities of temporal replaying and the repetition of historical events, ideas and identities.

PERFORMANCE, ROLE PLAY AND RE-ENACTMENT
Over the last decade and a half, Bronstein has framed the process by which he produces his beautifully rendered and expansive drawings as a form of role play. When drawing, he seeks to imagine himself as an 18th-century aristocratic architect in rural England or a radical protagonist of the 1970s Italian avant-garde. He suggests this might be understood as a way of expanding the frameworks within which he can work, moving beyond his own direct social experiences, disciplinary constraints and place in history. As he explains: 'Sometimes I take on the role of a commissioner, someone requesting a drawing and expecting a certain kind of drawing. At other times I play the architect – the time period the architect comes from, and quality of the architecture are of course for me to decide.' Bronstein can thus position himself to operate in different frames of mind to create work that society and the art-viewing public might not otherwise feel comfortable engaging with. For example, his explorations of despotic desire are manifest through the creation of large monumental structures, such as *Erecting of the Paternoster Square Column* (2008): 'The process allows me to "design" any building I want to – bad as well as good. It is architectural drawing at the service of historical comment.'

Pablo Bronstein,
European building from the 1990s subsequently redecorated and abandoned,
2016

A 1990s-style building overlaid with playful and idiotic Rococo-inspired decoration.

Role play is also used by Bronstein as a means to explore an 'internal universe' to justify his personal obsessions within a public context: 'I work principally within and with found imagery, with particular references that are of interest really only to me or to a very, very small group of people.' However this is 'not just a practice exclusively seen as one that is art historical ... but representative of my desire to re-create and represent these references as an artistic act and as relevant to today'. Role play and performance enable him to create work based on his own esoteric interests as a legitimate art practice that celebrates his individual compulsions.

For Jacob, the terms 'enactment' and 're-enactment' describe a property inherent to architecture, in the sense that it is always either trying to act as something other than it actually is, or trying to make explicit what it is to both its context and history. This way of seeing and describing architecture stemmed from his appreciation of buildings with 'an obvious theatricality to them. What I especially liked was buildings that did the thing, but also showed you that they were doing that thing.' He notes how projects by Robert Venturi from the 1960s onwards, such as the Guild House retirement home (Philadelphia, 1963) with its golden TV antenna and centralised entrance column, 'make allusions to history while also existing in the present: performing a role while acknowledging the performance of that role and explicitly displaying the armatures and stagecraft.'

Jacob argues this also applies to the reading of Modernists such as Mies van der Rohe whom the experimental architects of the 1960s and 1970s were often reacting against. Van der Rohe's architecture was of course a language, but the repetition of this language across different projects (both his and those of others) means that for Jacob his buildings 'in some ways are always performing and re-performing themselves through repetition'.

Reflecting upon Jacob's idea of how a building can be seen as an enactment, Bronstein argues that you can 'understand the intention of a project, whether that's from the person who commissioned it or the ideology of the system within which it was commissioned', because it 'works on you, to organise you, as a form of control, prescribing what is permitted and what isn't permitted in any particular space'. Imagining the building as an enactment allows those occupying it to embark on their own process of 're-imagining their relationship with space, architecture or with the city, imagining other possible kinds of scenarios into the world you are occupying. Whether that's just through how you behave in a particular space, or how you add or subtract things from your physical experience of that world.'

Here, for both Jacob and Bronstein, we can start to consciously exercise the space of the cerebral – our interpretation of the world – into our actual experience of architecture. We become aware of our understanding of spaces and buildings when we are reading them and of our power to transform them for ourselves. This notion resonates with Jacob's proposition that 'if we equate the Modernist idea of function to performance or script then, say, cooking in a kitchen is performing according to the script. If you're having sex there, you're slightly off-script and the narrative of the space/occupation becomes a little more interesting. Our performance within spaces produces architectural meaning.' This is something that echoes with the origin of architecture: 'ancient sites like Stonehenge were in part built to host ritual and festival. Maybe the essential role of architecture is performance.'

Sam Jacob Studio,
A Very Small Part of Architecture,
Highgate Cemetery,
London,
2014

This project resurrected Adolf Loos's 1921 never-built mausoleum for Austrian Czech art historian Max Dvorak at 1:1 scale. Through a strategy of 'ghostly re-enactment', Jacob demonstrates the enduring influence of Loos's ideas upon modern architecture.

WE BECOME AWARE OF OUR UNDERSTANDING OF SPACES AND BUILDINGS WHEN WE ARE READING THEM AND OF OUR POWER TO TRANSFORM THEM FOR OURSELVES

RE-ENACTING THE AVANT-GARDE

The framing of role play, enactment and re-enactment in such a way establishes conceptual links emerging in the work of Bronstein and Jacob with that being produced by certain architects in the 1960s and 1970s, especially those understood as embodying the avant-garde. It also suggests new forms of process that move beyond historical referencing or the re-creation of historical tropes common in collage-based works towards a more methodological approach that seeks to understand their creation. Both Bronstein and Jacob have very particular and personal reasons for why the work of this period is so important as a reference point.

For Bronstein, the relationship emerged from an increasing awareness of the environments in London in which he was growing up in the 1980s: 'I grew up in Neasden where along stretches of rather boring roads, you would get warehouses of furniture and glazing that would look like impoverished versions of the stuff celebrated by Charles Jencks and his notions of *adhocism*.'[1] It was later, at art school, that he discovered the possible origin of these forms in Rossi and Venturi. Rossi's quiet radicalism, for example in his Teatro del Mundo designed for the Venice Architecture Biennale in 1979, was particularly influential: 'I was amazed by his floating theatre; it seemed to embody this idea that architecture could be seriously f*cked with. It still feels like a radical gesture, despite the fact that its image has become so present in architectural culture.' The dissonance between the theatre as a typology and the act of floating 'felt like it was ripping something out and putting it somewhere else'.

Jacob's introduction to re-enaction was born of the economic necessity that accompanied the early period of his work as part of FAT, the practice he co-founded in the 1990s and directed with Sean Griffiths and Charles Holland until 2013. FAT's now famous Postmodern style partly emerged as a result of the typical pressures any young practice would face: 'We had a job converting an old chapel. At the time we wanted to build a blob on sticks as a floating bedroom. It was way too expensive and somehow we changed tack and built a fake barn facade instead – a completely opposite approach.' Another experience that reinforced this nascent interest was when he 'accidentally discovered Venturi in a bargain bookshop on Upper Street' in Islington, London. The power of the work came in regarding it in a modern setting, which was 'enlightening to study in the context of the mid-1990s'. In an age 'where the Internet was taking off and communication, advertising and media were so pervasive,' Venturi and Denise Scott Brown's seminal writings such as 1972's *Learning from Las Vegas*,[2] and their work together as Venturi, Scott Brown & Associates did not seem historical, but sparked a contemporary reaction: 'It was like wow, that's a really good idea! Billboards are architecture too.'

Bronstein's and Jacob's engagement with the avant-garde was a means to start to understand the work they were directly producing, experiencing and acting within. At the time, within the schools both were studying at, figures such as Rossi and particularly Venturi were controversial, lending their concepts an illicit charge by sailing against the prevailing winds of Deconstructivism and early computation. Bronstein's and Jacob's development of these ideas in a context that was out-of-step, both intellectually and historically, began in the formative stage of their careers and led to the unique position of their work.

Pablo Bronstein,
Plaza Monument,
2006

In this 1980s-style drawing of a monument, Postmodern walls are supported by Doric columns to form a courtyard ensemble within a Neoclassical border.

Pablo Bronstein,
Bright New Façade,
2011

Bronstein's 18th-century-inspired perspectival illustration of a decontextualised building with unsophisticated but pretentious surface ornamentation is clumsily augmented by crude hand-colouring.

AVANT-GARDE AS PROVOCATION

Both Bronstein's and Jacob's works can be seen as touchstones of the increasing re-engagement with the philosophies of Rossi and Venturi, as well as those who followed them into the Postmodern canon. Bronstein's career has now spanned nearly 15 years, and included exhibitions at venues such as the Metropolitan Museum in New York (2009) and Tate Britain (2016) in London. Jacob's work grew alongside his practice FAT and subsequently his own studio, with his influence extending into academic positions as Professor at the University of Illinois at Chicago and his regular columns in the wider design press. In both cases, the reintroduction of these influences into established hegemonies that had no place for them was done with much gusto, and performed as a provocation. Such a process reverberates with the ambitions of their historical forebears.

As Jacob recounts, this literally placed them in an avant-garde position, in advance of other practices and designers who have subsequently taken up the mantle of neo-Postmodernism: 'Nobody else was doing that kind of thing. We weren't even doing that kind of thing for a long time.' And more than simply a design language, it was a different way of understanding architecture's role in the world, as well as what might constitute an expanded notion of architectural practice.

Role play, enactment and re-enactment were used by both Jacob and Bronstein throughout the last two decades as operations to reference the past and make work that spoke about the present. In developing his approach, Bronstein used certain references to directly challenge notions of what art practice should be. It was an attempt to challenge an art world too focused on self-consciously social projects: 'The artist Stephen Willats was having a revival at the time, and a fair amount of work was being made about people not being able to get their shopping trolley up council-flat steps. Parallel to this there was an astonishingly vapid celebration of Modernism.' In contrast, with regard to his own interests, Bronstein states that 'within the art world, Postmodern architecture was extraordinarily unfashionable and completely invisible as a reference point', which led to his work being misunderstood as 'celebratory of high finance and previous booms'. It was this condition that Bronstein was trying to challenge to question blunt associations between Postmodernism and historicism and contest popular assumptions of the time about the relationship between taste and capital, fantasy and reality.

Sam Jacob Studio,
Chicago Pasticcio,
Chicago Architecture Biennial,
2017

Pasticcio is a design for a tower composed of varied architectural references fused into a new whole: a new kind of tower made from fragments of history. Drawing from Loos's 1922 Tribune Tower competition entry alongside the selected Howells and Hood scheme, it involves re-enacting a new, alternative history.

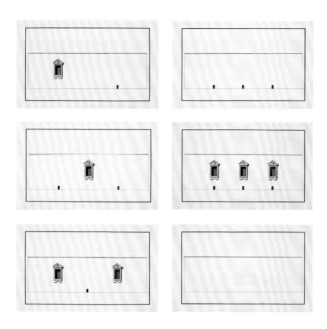

Pablo Bronstein,
Primitive facade variations,
2014

Early 19th-century French-style facade
drawings with varying configurations
of heavy Mannerist windows and plain
arched door apertures, wall and cornice.

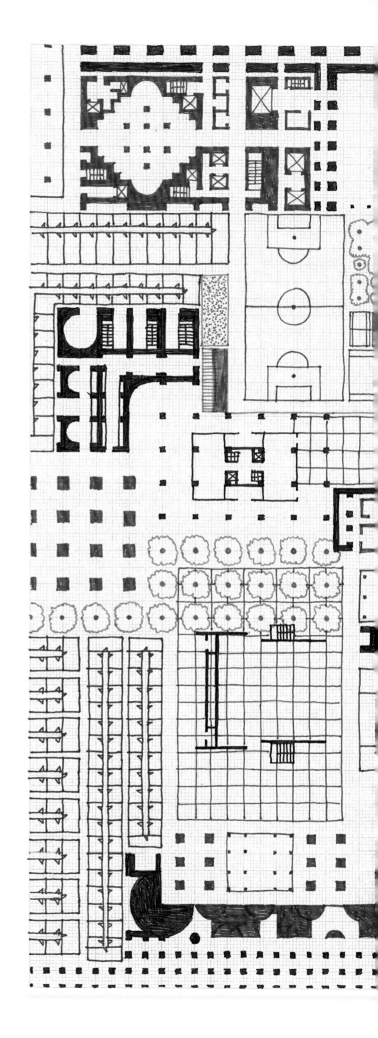

BY 'PLAYING IT AGAIN', THEY CONTINUE TO DEVELOP METHODOLOGIES TOWARDS AND AGAINST A HISTORY OF THE AVANT-GARDE

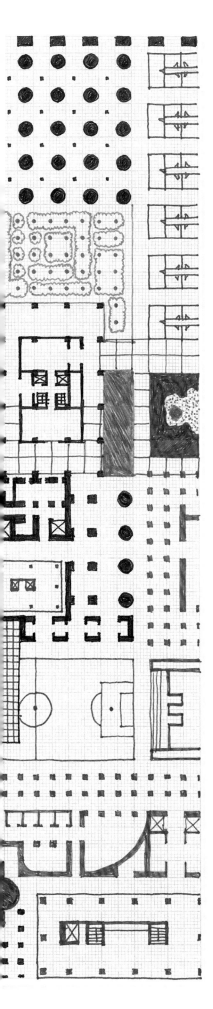

Sam Jacob Studio,
Empire of Ice Cream,
2014–

Drawing from a series exploring an expressionistic doodled mega-plan, an unconscious graphic of territory in which castles, housing, football pitches, sewage works and grand pianos merge into a non-stop landscape of architecture.

Sam Jacob Studio,
One Thing After Another,
2016

Drawing featuring a garden shed, a 3D-scanned and overscaled CNC version and a 3D-printed smaller version of the same shed.

The critical position of Jacob's architecture was aimed directly at the repackaging of Britain's identity as a truly modern state under the leadership of Tony Blair: 'New Labour brought with it a new aesthetic of Scandi-Modernism, a new kind of good taste for a we-are-all-middle-class-now era.' Following philosophies of Venturi and Scott Brown, Jacob, along with his compatriots at FAT, instead looked at the edges of culture – and 'bad' taste especially: 'I suppose we liked things like chintz because it contained so much other stuff – things to do with class and cultural value – and so gave us a means to make work that addressed political ideas through aesthetics.' Venturi and Scott Brown's avant-garde project, like that of FAT, was to probe the extents of cultural production and how that could become architecture: 'What interested us was the fact that they'd been looking at "ugly" stuff, playing games trying to outdo each other by each liking something more horrible than the other. I found this notion of stretching – or even suspending – one's own personal taste regime really productive.'

Both Bronstein and Jacob have integrated the re-enactment of avant-garde tropes and ideals into their practice. Their work sits apart from its contemporaries by provoking, re-imagining and reshaping contradictions that challenge history as a sequential set of proceedings and question the notion of architecture as a discipline with finite and fixed boundaries. By 'playing it again', they continue to develop methodologies towards and against a history of the avant-garde. ⌂

This article is based on a conversation between Matthew Butcher and Luke Pearson, and Sam Jacob and Pablo Bronstein at Bronstein's East London home and studio in November 2018.

Notes
1. Charles Jencks, *Adhocism: The Case for Improvisation*, Doubleday (New York), 1972.
2. Robert Venturi, Denise Scott Brown and Steven Izenour, *Learning from Las Vegas*, MIT Press (Cambridge MA), 1972.

Text © 2019 John Wiley & Sons Ltd. Images: pp 100, 103, 105(b), 106-7(c), 107(r) © Sam Jacob; p 101 Courtesy the artist and Herald St, London, photo Hugo Glendinning; pp 102, 104, 105(t) Courtesy the artist and Herald St, London; p 106(l) Courtesy the artist; Herald St, London and Galleria Franco Noero, Turin

ARCHITECTURE BETWEEN THE PANELS

COMICS, CARTOONS AND GRAPHIC NARRATIVE IN THE (NEW) NEO AVANT-GARDE

Avant-garde architects from the 1960s onwards drew numerous outside influences into the discipline, reshaping architecture's limits and communicative properties. Architect and researcher **Luis Miguel Lus Arana**, lecturer in History and Theory of Architecture at the University of Zaragoza in Spain, explores how comic books and cartoons were mobilised by groups such as Archigram, Ant Farm and Utopie to experiment with space and time. This discussion is accompanied by a specially commissioned comic by Lus Arana's alter ego, the cartoonist **Klaus**, charting this avant-garde path from the experimental architecture of the mid-20th century to the protagonists of today.

Klaus,
*The Comics of the Avant-Garde (I):
Space, Time, Anarchitecture,*
2018

The introduction of evolution, change, flexibility, ephemerality and, ultimately, *time* as an element of design prompted the use of graphic narrative in its different forms, either to explain the way projects work, or, eventually, to provide it with a fictional background. On this page, some of Archigram's forays into 'sequential narrative' (*Instant City Airship Sequence*, 1970; *The Metamorphosis of Our Town*, 1970; *Plug-In University Node*, 1965; *House 1990*, 1965; *House of the Seven Veils*, 1974), and one page of Mark Fisher's *The Adventures of Amersham 'Arry* (1970–71), a series of fictional stories that presented the many uses of his *Dynamat* project.

The 1960s, best represented in the collective imagination by the events that surrounded the civil unrest in France in May 1968, witnessed a general shake-up of established structures. Always vindictive and eager to abolish the traditional borders between 'hi' and 'lo', popular and official, 'light' and mature, the younger generations embraced the colourful products of culture's lower strata. The 1960s were also a time where comics entered academia – through the works of filmmakers such as Jean-Luc Godard and Alain Resnais, and intellectuals such as Umberto Eco, or, slightly less enthusiastically, Marshall McLuhan – and simultaneously went underground. Comic books explored anti-establishment niches and re-conquered the mainstream, through new superheroes whose cosmic adventures entered colleges populated by a generation experimenting with mind-expanding drugs. Comics were

everywhere, aided by an emerging independent publishing scene that made extensive use of them, as the embodiment of the spirit of an age characterised by a mixture of provocation and ingenuity, neo-Marxism and stark individualism, hedonistic *laissez-faire* and political activism.

Unsurprisingly, the proliferating architectural 'little magazines' of the 1960s and early 1970s, which embraced the same guerrilla tactics of appropriation of the goodies of popular culture, also featured comics prominently. They were used for their subversive value, their ability for image-shaping, their advantages for communication, or a combination of all of these. The London-based group Archigram championed this trend in *Archigram 4* (1964), a manifesto on the ability of science fiction to prefigure the shape of a new architecture which, in full Situationist

Klaus,
*The Comics of the Avant-Garde (II):
Fun and Fiction,*
2018

Comics became an even more useful tool the more projects departed from the permanent built object, be it because they had an indefinable shape, or because they belonged in the realm of fiction. On this page, DIY structures by Stuart Lever (*Tree Project*, 1970–71), biologically developed structures by Rudolf Doernach (*Provolution*, 1968) and Mark Fisher (*Les Aventures de M Nemo de Bonpland*, 1974), and a reality populated by sentient cars in Piers Gough, Philip Wagner and Diana Jowsey's *Motorolorama* (1970–71).

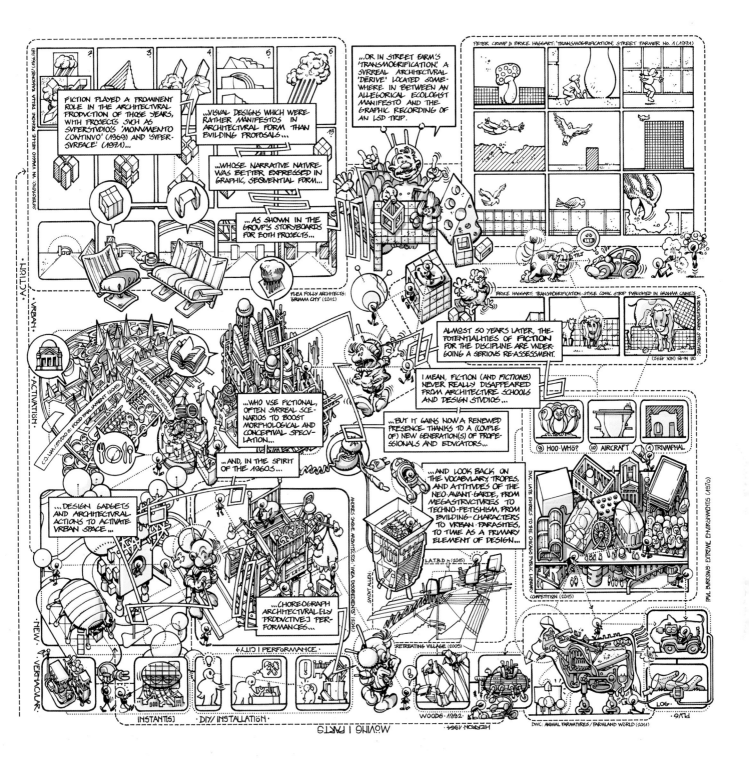

Klaus,
The Comics of the Avant-Garde (III):
Fictions,
2018

At the top, some examples of architecture (in comic-strip
form) as a way to convey a message, either political, as in
Superstudio's storyboards for their *Continuous Monument*
(1969) project, or surrealistically ecological, as in Street Farm's
several *Transmogrifications* (1971). At the bottom, some
contemporary practices which use fiction as a trigger for
designs that end up formally echoing those of the 1960s–70s:
FleaFollyArchitects, CJ Lim / Atelier 8, WE ARE AN EVENT,
Andrés Jaque / Office for Political Innovation, Smout Allen,
Design With Company.

fashion, was profusely illustrated with space comics.[1] Soon this
use of comics by appropriation became a staple of the period's
avant-garde: San Francisco collective Ant Farm's DIY guide
INFLATOCOOKBOOK (1971),[2] the early issues (1967–9) of
the eponymous journal of the Paris-based Utopie group and their
related publications such as *Urbaniser la lutte de classe* (1969),[3]
and even Paul Krassner and Ken Kesey's *Last Supplement* to
American writer Stewart Brand's ecologist *Whole Earth Catalog*
(1971), together with an endless array of student journals, give a
good account of this.

However, appropriation and insertion for caustic effect was
not the only way in which comics made it into the architectural
avant-garde. The 1960s were also a period where megastructures
finally disintegrated in a nebula of capsules, cells, mobile units

Klaus,
*The Comics of the Avant-Garde (IV):
The New Neo,*
2018

An overview of the use of graphic narrative by some
contemporary practices: Steven McCloy, Design With
Company, Jones & Partners, Luke Pearson, Jimenez Lai /
Bureau Spectacular, Mitnick.Roddier.

and inflatable structures. Objects gave way to architectural actions, form to performance, and in this new context of 'architecture without architecture', graphic narrative revealed a powerful representation tool. Archigram used it profusely in many projects where time was an inherent component of the design, such as *Instant City* (1968–70) and *Metamorphosis of an English Town* (1970), and it became even more relevant when architecture was the result of a process of unpredictable form, as in Rudolf Doernach's bio-tectural *Provolution* (1966),[4] an 'architectural *dérive*' akin to an LSD trip, as in Street Farm's different 'transmogrifications' (1971),[5] or simply a political statement, as in Superstudio's various storyboards (1966–9).

· FROM LEFT TO RIGHT: SIR PETER COOK, STEVEN McCLOY (IN DISGUISE), STEWART HICKS AND ALLISON NEWMEYER (DESIGN WITH COMPANY), C.J. LIM (STUDIO 8), MARK SMOUT, LAURA ALLEN, LUKE PEARSON, WES JONES (JONES, PARTNERS: ARCHITECTURE), KLAUS (KLAUSTOON), LUIS MIGUEL (KOLDO) LUS-ARANA, KEITH MITNICK, MIREILLE RODDIER, JIMENEZ LAI (BUREAU SPECTACULAR), ALEX CULLEN AND DANNY TRAVIS (ARCHITECTURE HERO), PHINEAS THE FLY (BEAUTIFULLY BANAL). [FAMILY PIC WITH SOME OF THE PEOPLE FEATURED THROUGHOUT THE ARTICLE]. FOR A MORE DETAILED RECOUNT OF THE INTERACTIONS OF GRAPHIC NARRATIVE AND CONTEMPORARY PRACTICES, PLEASE REFER TO: 'COMICS AND ARCHITECTURE: A READING GUIDE', CHAPTER 20 IN JONATHAN CHARLEY'S THE ROUTLEDGE COMPANION ON ARCHITECTURE, LITERATURE AND THE CITY (ROUTLEDGE, 2018).

Five decades later, the changes faced by the profession, paired with the shift of cultural paradigm brought about by the digital revolution, are fostering a paradoxical comeback, with renewed strength and augmented potentialities, of the old-school, low-tech *arte povera* of comics. Fiction – an ineludible component of architectural design that gave us some excellent architectural comics by the likes of Mark Fisher, Stuart Lever and Philip Wagner during Archigram co-founder Peter Cook's tenure as 5th-year studio instructor at the Architectural Association in London[6] – has been re-entering the schools, often paired with comics, as a pedagogical tool. Even more significantly, fiction today is re-entering architectural offices by the hand of younger practices – FleaFollyArchitects in London, Design With Company in Chicago, WE ARE AN EVENT in Mexico City, or Office for Political Innovation in Madrid, to name just a few. Free from the building anxiety of the millennium bubble, these new practices reconnect with the spirit of the 1960s neo avant-garde, producing theoretical designs, performances and installations which take up their strategies, shticks, general stylistic signatures, graphic philosophies and, sometimes, their means of representation. In an age of fast communication and mediated digital imaging, slow-paced, handcrafted comics are a useful tool to communicate designs in an accessible way, and with an added visual punch, but also to develop the designs themselves. The graphic and narrative medium of comics provides an alternative reality that helps construct design narratives, and sometimes can even be used as a formalising device. This is the case with architect Jimenez Lai, founder of Los Angeles-based office Bureau Spectacular, whose short stories often play with the conflation of time and space, amalgamating panels and page layouts in a sort of automatic shaping process that overlaps with his built work.

Beyond their role as a companion to design, comics have recently started being vindicated as an end in themselves. Increasingly, we find architect-produced comics intended solely as 'architecture fiction', as manifestos, as a vehicle for architecture discourses, critique or satire. If the late 2000s saluted the advent of architecture fiction as a concept, works such as Beijing-based Drawing Architecture Studio's series of research-turned-books *A Little Bit of Beijing* (2013–18),[7] and *Beautifully Banal* (2016) by Chicago studio Architecture Hero (Danny Travis and Alexander Culler),[8] rank amongst the first entries of a new genre, the architectural graphic novel: comics for architects done by architects that hint, perhaps, at a new practice field for a profession in desperate need of re-invention.

But that's a different story. ᗫ

Notes
1. Peter Cook (ed), *Archigram no 4: Zoom Issue*, May 1964. An analysis of these space comics can be found in: Luis Miguel Lus Arana, 'Building a utopie autre [Amazing Archigram! – 50 years of Zoom!/ Zzzzrrtt!/ Thud!/ Blaam!]', *Proyecto, Progreso, Arquitectura*, 11, 2014, pp 90–103.
2. Ant Farm, *INFLATOCOOKBOOK*, Ant Farm (Sausalito, CA), 1971
3. Utopie, *Urbaniser la lutte de classe*, Éditions Utopie (Paris), 1969.
4. See ᗫ, February 1966 (vol 36), p 96.
5. See, for instance: Bruce Haggart, 'Transmogrification', *Street Farmer*, September (no 1), 1971, unpaginated.
6. See Peter Cook, 'The Electric Decade: An Atmosphere at the AA School, 1963–1973', in James Gowan (ed.), *A Continuous Experiment: Learning and Teaching at the Architectural Association*, AA (London), 1975, pp 137–44.
7. The series, each volume focusing on a different district of Beijing, is by Li Han and Hu Yan and published by Tongji University Press.
8. Alexander Culler and Danny Travis, *The Complete Beautifully Banal: An Architectural Graphic Trilogy*, Lowitz + Sons (Chicago), 2015.

THE GRAPHIC AND NARRATIVE MEDIUM OF COMICS PROVIDES AN ALTERNATIVE REALITY THAT HELPS CONSTRUCT DESIGN NARRATIVES

Text © 2019 John Wiley & Sons Ltd.
Images by Klaus (www.klaustoon.wordpress.com)

COPYING AS CULTURAL ICONOCLASM

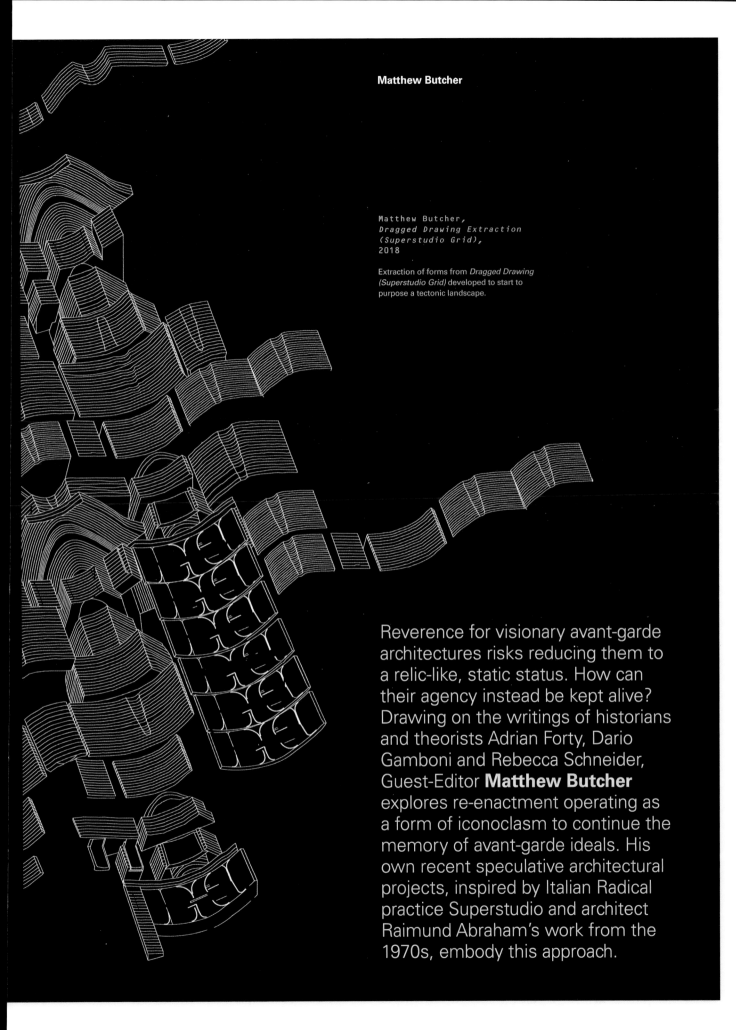

Matthew Butcher

Matthew Butcher,
*Dragged Drawing Extraction
(Superstudio Grid)*,
2018

Extraction of forms from *Dragged Drawing
(Superstudio Grid)* developed to start to
purpose a tectonic landscape.

Reverence for visionary avant-garde architectures risks reducing them to a relic-like, static status. How can their agency instead be kept alive? Drawing on the writings of historians and theorists Adrian Forty, Dario Gamboni and Rebecca Schneider, Guest-Editor **Matthew Butcher** explores re-enactment operating as a form of iconoclasm to continue the memory of avant-garde ideals. His own recent speculative architectural projects, inspired by Italian Radical practice Superstudio and architect Raimund Abraham's work from the 1970s, embody this approach.

If the popular cultural consensus and understanding of architecture is predominantly centred on the process of building, as opposed to the wider forms of the discipline such as writing and drawing, then the notion of architecture as a philosophical or artistic endeavour is not being forefronted as much as it should be.

As a resistance to this condition, the series of recent projects explored here attempt to re-enact an architectural avant-garde, and in particular a late or neo avant-garde from the 1960s and 1970s – 'a moment in history', as described by theorist K Michael Hays, 'when certain ways of practicing architecture still had philosophical aspirations'.[1] This re-enactment, manifested as drawings of speculative architectural projects, aims to reflect the look and essence of the work of the avant-garde of the period.

There is, of course, a problem within this ambition – one that resonates with what art theorist Peter Burger set out in his seminal text *Theory of the Avant-Garde* (1982), against the work of the neo avant-garde of the 1960s and 1970s. He argues that the tendency of this later avant-garde work to repeat formal and conceptual tropes of the historical avant-garde of the early 20th century was not a valuable practice; that the repetition seen in this newer work could not replicate the initial levels of shock propagated by movements such as Dada and Surrealism; and that cultural institutions, ending the ability of these modes of practice to disrupt existing cultural hegemonies, had already absorbed the forms of practice seen in this newer work.[2]

To counteract this potential problem – that re-enactment could be considered a kind of iconophilia, a reverence for past images and artefacts – the recent design work featured in this article explores how a form of iconoclasm can instead be incorporated through the act of repetition. The use of iconoclasm within the context of re-enactment can be seen as a means of provoking debate on the role and purpose of any avant-garde without seeking to duplicate it, where iconoclasm can be understood as the desire to wipe out or distort specific historical ideas through the destruction of certain art or architectures, or through the act of their debasement. The aim here is to seek to contextualise this work in certain theoretical and historical contexts. These include the writings of architectural historian Adrian Forty and art historian Dario Gamboni, and in certain notions of re-enactment put forward by performance theorist Rebecca Schneider.

Iconoclasm as an Act of Memorial
In the introduction to his book *The Art of Forgetting* (1999), Adrian Forty sets out to address what he sees as the failure in 20th-century architectural theory and practice to truly embody cultural, political or individual memories. He states that 'In architecture and urbanism, we find a particularly striking case of a persisting and almost wholly uncritical attachment to the traditional Western belief that material objects – in this case building – provide a complete and satisfactory analogue for the mental world of memory' that is formed from an 'Aristotelian-based assumption that to transfer memories to objects would preserve them from mental decay'.[3] As a riposte to this condition, Forty argues instead that any art wishing to engage with ideas of memory must also engage with the process of forgetting.[4]

Within this context he refers directly to the acts of iconoclasm which, more often than not, can strengthen certain cultural, political or social memories while also engaging in a process of trying to forget them. He goes on to state that iconoclasm does not necessarily lessen memory; instead it has tended to perpetuate it.[5] In addition to this premise, Forty refers to Paul Connerton's analysis on memory in his book *How Societies Remember* (1989) and argues that 'material objects have less significance in perpetuating memory' than, amongst other temporal situations, 'rituals' and 'embodied acts'.[6]

As an echo to Forty's argument, Dario Gamboni, in his text 'Image to Destroy, Indestructible Image' (2002), sets out the idea that iconoclasm should not be seen as purely a destructive act, and that there is a symbiotic relationship between iconophilia and iconoclasm.[7] Gamboni states that 'The gesture of aggression itself, in retrospect or seen from a different perspective, can reveal itself to be a gesture of reverence – and vice versa.'[8] He highlights several historical precedents where the action of iconoclasm was a means to reinstate certain historic artworks as an active agent in the world, as opposed to celebrated relics sat static in a museum.[9] For Gamboni the iconoclast in these cases was working against the sanctity placed on the 'unique' art object, and the commercial value that is then applied to it.[10] As part of this discussion he presents the avant-garde and neo-avant-garde debasement of reproductions of famous artworks, such as Fluxus artist Daniel Spoerri's use of an image of Leonardo Da Vinci's *Mona Lisa* (1503) as an ironing-board cover in his work *Use a Rembrandt as an Ironing Board* (Marcel Duchamp) (1964), and Asger Jorn's encouragement to his colleagues in COBRA – an art movement that was operating from the late 1940s to the early 1950s – to improve paintings and museum collections, stating 'paint over the pictures to preserve their actuality and to help them from falling into oblivion'.[11]

Re-enactment as Reverence and Remembrance
Rebecca Schneider, in her book *Performing Remains: Art and War in Times of Theatrical Reenactment* (2011), suggests that 'the experience of reenactment [...] is an intense, embodied enquiry into temporal repetition, temporal recurrence'.[12] The term for Schneider refers to 'the practice of re-playing or redoing a precedent event, artwork or act'.[13] Artists associated with these ideas include Pablo Bronstein (see the article on pp 100–107 of this issue of *D*), who role-plays certain characters or historical archetypes when he draws, which is used as a distinct methodology to create complex and fantastical environments. It also can be seen in the work of artist Goshka Macuga, who reconstructed one of Kasimir Malevich's *Arkhitectons* in *Arkhitectony – After K Malevich* (2005), giving them a scale and function which Malevich did not originally intend; an action that seeks to repurpose the meaning of the original work within a contemporary context.[14]

These artists, and the works associated with them, not only operate as distortions of linear temporality but also aim to undermine the cult of the singular art object, a particular condition reinforced by museum collections. The methodologies of re-enactment, and the notions of mimesis

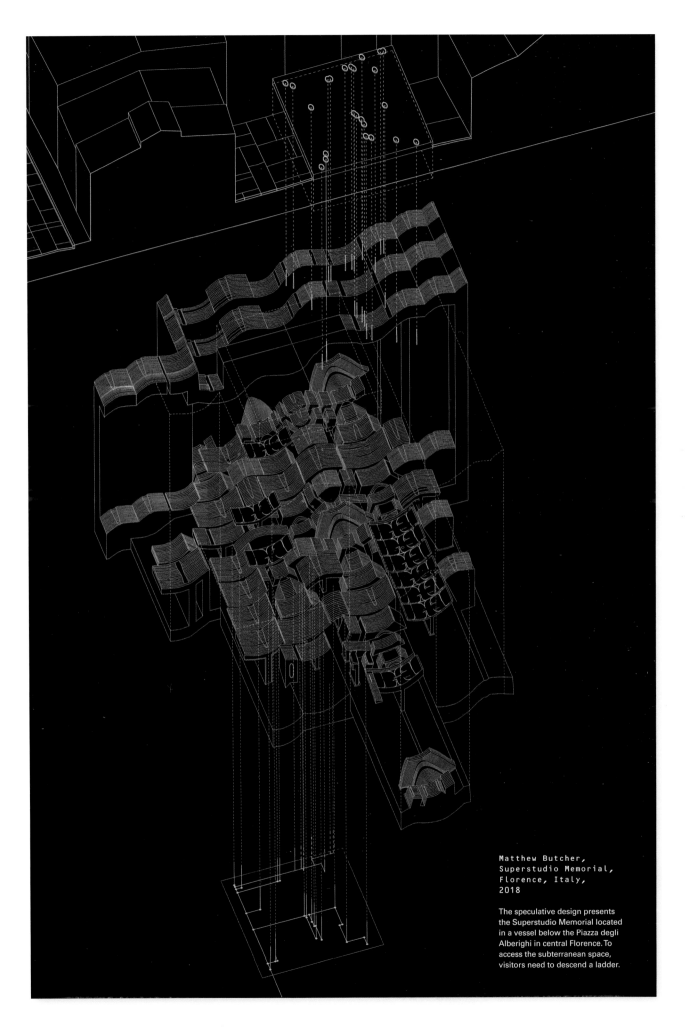

Matthew Butcher,
Superstudio Memorial,
Florence, Italy,
2018

The speculative design presents
the Superstudio Memorial located
in a vessel below the Piazza degli
Alberighi in central Florence. To
access the subterranean space,
visitors need to descend a ladder.

and theatricality that are associated with it, are, as Schneider notes, 'not threats to authenticity, but, like language itself, vehicles for access to the transitive, performative and cross temporal real'.[15] Here, events, objects, historical styles and artefacts exist in a never-ending process of reinvention and re-contextualisation; a continuous memorialisation.

Echoes and Distortions of the Avant-Garde

There are two ways in which the recent design work illustrated here seeks to build a reciprocity with the avant-garde of the 1960s and 1970s, through a process that could be understood as re-enactment that acts as both iconophily and iconoclasm.

The first of these could be said to exist in a speculative proposal for a monument to the work of radical avant-garde protagonists Superstudio. The monument, a grotto-like space for personal reflection, sits below Piazza degli Alberighi in the historic centre of Florence, Italy. The structure consists of an oval room with a concrete undulating floor, providing space for resting, walking and sitting. This central platform takes its form from a specific design methodology that utilises a process of digital scanning.

To create this act of iconoclasm, a reproduction of one of Superstudio's drawings was dragged across the surface of an image scanner while it was in the process of being scanned. The subsequent work *Dragged Drawing (Superstudio Grid)* (2015) is a direct mapping of this action and the scanning process – a physical imprint of the drawing as it moves through time and space. Out of this new materialisation of the original Superstudio image, a series of forms were identified, tracing various contours, then spliced out.

The design is also informed by another image distortion of the original Superstudio grid – where the drawing was photocopied and recopied until it all but disappears, apart from a few marks and dots. These dots then inform the location on the main floor plate where hot air is piped to heat the space. The dots are also used to define a network of holes located in the concrete ceiling, which allow tiny drops of water to form Calthemites there after collecting minerals from the concrete structure while passing through it.

These processes of image distortion could be linked to sampling in music, where a digital copy is taken from an existing audio recording and can then be manipulated and reproduced in different ways. Although a clear distortion of the original image, this action could be seen as an attempt to draw out an essence of the original sampled architectures; an intrinsic formal and aesthetic logic from the original source that can be carried forward to another time and place. In this case, the re-imagining of the Superstudio grid is open to different constellations of meanings.

The second process linked to understandings of re-enactment can be seen within the Silt House (2015), Silt House Chapel (2014) and Bang Bang House (2016), projects that propose speculative future dwellings and structures that present a series of practical and poetic investigations into the inhabitation of a future flooded Thames Estuary.[16]

Matthew Butcher,
*Dragged Drawing
(Superstudio Grid)*,
2015

To create the image, a reproduction of Superstudio's drawing of the Misura Furniture Series from 1969–70 was dragged across the surface of an image scanner while it was in the process of being scanned.

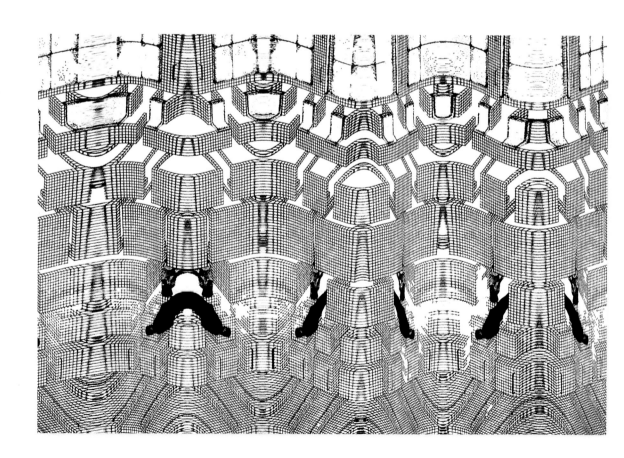

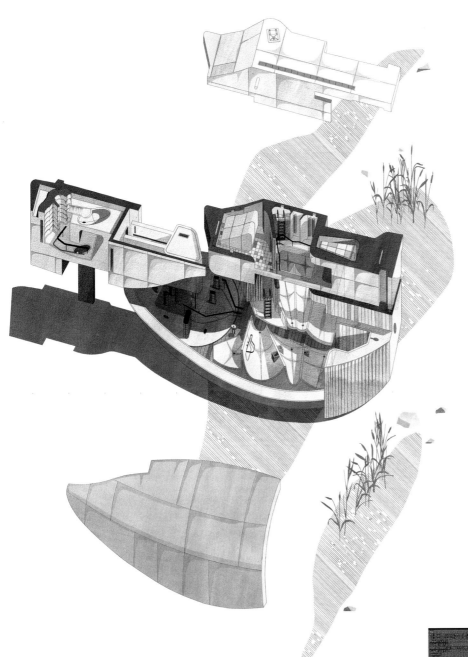

Matthew Butcher,
Silt House,
Cliffe Marshes,
Thames Estuary,
UK,
2015

Future dwelling that presents a practical and poetic investigation into the inhabitation of a future flooded Thames Estuary. The forms are derived from an interpretation of the work of Raimund Abraham, such as in his House with Curtains (1971).

Animation stills from an aerial plan, formed using particle modelling software, show how the build-up of sediment would form over and around the Silt House.

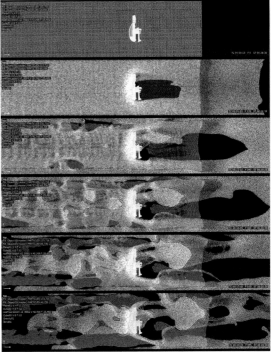

In this case, the re-imagining of the Superstudio grid is open to different constellations of meanings

Matthew Butcher,
Silt House Chapel,
Cliffe Marshes,
Thames Estuary,
UK,
2014

Part of the Silt House project for the Thames Estuary, the Silt House Chapel – shown here in an exploded isometric digital collage – features forms derived from the 2015 *Dragged Drawing* of Superstudio's Misura Furniture Series from 1969–70 and an interpretation of the work of Raimund Abraham.

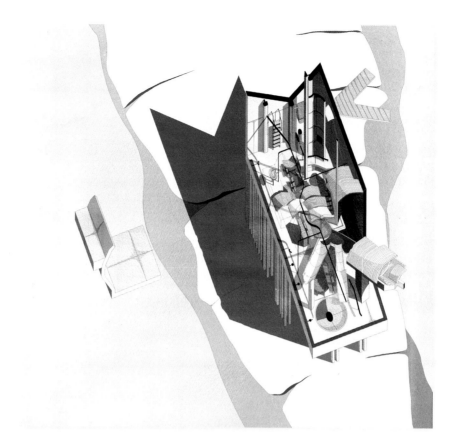

The repetition of one style or historical reference, and the disruption and distortion of an original drawing, can be seen as an act of iconoclasm

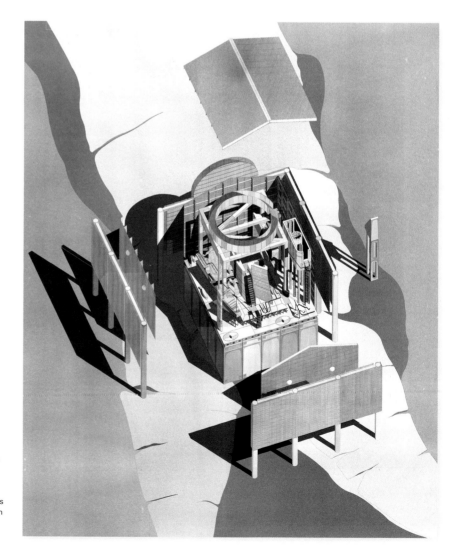

Matthew Butcher,
Bang Bang House,
Canvey Island,
Thames Estuary,
UK,
2016

The Bang Bang House, a floating structure, has its location altered continually by the moving currents of the Estuary. Like the Silt House Chapel, it also contains formal elements which have been extracted from the Superstudio *Dragged Drawings*.

Raimund Abraham,
House with Curtains,
1971

The sketch shows the design for House with
Curtains, one of the structures that made
up Abraham's 10 Houses project (1970–73),
a series of speculative dwellings Abraham
designed that are located in a barren and
non-specific landscape.

Alongside the main function and narrative, the works also deliberately attempt to embody the spirit of avant-garde architect Raimund Abraham, and in particular his 10 Houses project from 1970–73, which he developed as illustrations of a series of dwellings located in, and forming part of, a disparate and barren landscape.

Through an analysis of 10 Houses, a visual grammar was garnered, defined by certain tropes that appear across the different buildings in this project. This includes buildings that are buried and the use of shapes that are reminiscent of natural forms. This 'grammar' was then used to inform key design ideas and logics of Silt House, Silt House Chapel and Bang Bang House.

For instance, the forms synonymous with cloud formations that are located in the basement of Abraham's Earth-Cloud House (1970) from his 10 Houses project can be seen in both Silt House and Silt House Chapel, not as miasma but as ridges that reverberate with the forms mud takes on following the movements of tidal currents across it. In another design from the 10 Houses project, House with Curtains (1971), we see the billowing fabrics rise up, deforming the house's gridded structure and thus presenting the idea that the weather and wind are materials which form the house as much as the glass and concrete of which it is proposed to be made. This motif is reflected in the design of the Silt House, where the form of the structure is conceived to allow water to flow around and over it, and for mud to settle on it. In the Bang Bang House, we see it reflected in the proposal for the design to float while moored within a metal rectangular dock. As the structure is moved from side to side and up and down by the shifting tide of the river, its specific location on the mud flat would be altered, and it would continually bang against the metal dock to which it is moored, creating sound that would echo through the structure when afloat. This specific ephemeral condition would be significant in making up the material experience of the house. Lastly, within the Silt House Chapel we are presented with a structure which is open to the Estuary's tidal waters. As water flows through the structure, sediment is deposited on and within the undulating concrete components of the Chapel's floor, again contributing to the material make-up of the architecture alongside the main concrete structure.

A Monument to Recurrence

By considering re-enactment as a distinctive design strategy, and drawing as a temporal action, we can distort traditional precepts of time and need for historical certainty. The repetition of one style or historical reference, and the disruption and distortion of an original drawing, can be seen as an act of iconoclasm. Through this iconoclasm we can aim not to destroy the memory of a historical architecture such as the late or neo avant-garde, but instead create an ongoing memorial and reverence without the sanctity of history taking precedence. ◠

Notes
1. K Michael Hays, *Architecture's Desire: Reading the Late Avant-Garde*, MIT Press (Cambridge, MA), 2010, p 2.
2. Peter Burger, *Theory of the Avant-Garde*, trans Michael Shaw, University of Minnesota Press (Minneapolis), 1984, pp 109 and 61.
3. Adrian Forty, 'Introduction', in Adrian Forty and Susanne Kucher (eds), *The Art of Forgetting*, Berg (Oxford), 1999, pp 13–15.
4. *Ibid*, p 16.
5. *Ibid*, p 12.
6. *Ibid*, p 2.
7. Dario Gamboni, 'Image to Destroy, Indestructible Image', in Bruno Latour and Peter Weibel (eds), *Iconoclash: Beyond the Image Wars in Science, Religion, and Art*, exhibition catalogue, ZKM-Center for Art and Media, Karlsruhe, Germany, MIT Press (Cambridge, MA and London), 2002, pp 88–135.
8. *Ibid*, p 88.
9. *Ibid*, pp 120–31.
10. *Ibid*, p 90.
11. *Ibid*, p 124. Quote originally taken from: Troels Andersson, *Asger Jorn: en Biografi, Årene 1914–53*, Borgen (Copenhagen), 1994.
12. Rebecca Schneider, *Performing Remains: Art and War in Times of Theatrical Reenactment*, Routledge (Abingdon), 2011, pp 1–2.
13. *Ibid*, p 2.
14. See Alan Colquhoun, *Modern Architecture*, Oxford University Press (Oxford), 2002, p 123.
15. Schneider, *op cit*, p 30.
16. For more detail on the poetic content of Silt House, see: Matthew Butcher, 'A Lyrical Architecture of the Flood: Landscape, Infrastructure and Symbiosis', *Architectural Research Quarterly*, 19 (3), 2015, pp 224–33.

Text © 2019 John Wiley & Sons Ltd. Images: pp 114-20 © Matthew Butcher; p 121 © Private collection Una Abraham

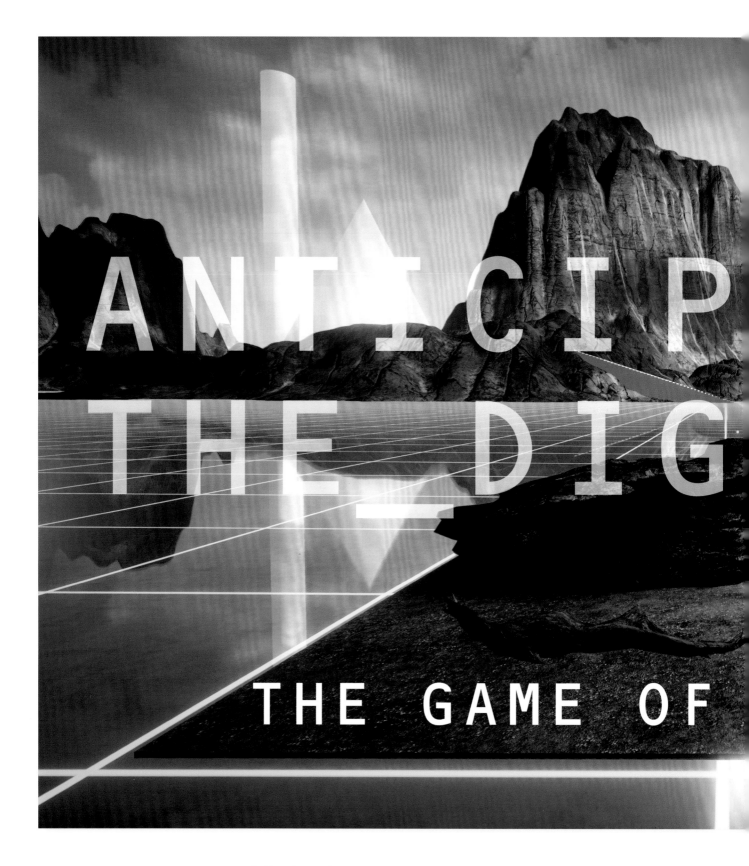

ANTICIP
THE_DIG
THE GAME OF

Damjan Jovanovic,
Supersurface computer game,
2016

In the Supersurface computer game, the player becomes a visitor to the world of Superstudio. The initial view of the game world repeats the theme of endless horizon and establishes clear vertical markers to guide the player.

ATING
ITAL_

SUPERSURFACE

Damjan Jovanovic

One of the many legacies left by the work of Superstudio was their iconic grid, which stands not only as a visual trope but as a prescient prediction of the way digital tools organise space. **Damjan Jovanovic** – an architect, educator and software designer based at the Southern California Institute of Architecture (SCI-Arc) in Los Angeles – discusses the importance of Superstudio's grid in relation to his computer-game environment Supersurface, which is a virtual re-creation of the Italian group's proto-digital collage environments.

It is quite possible that in 1972, Superstudio presented the first compelling image of the coming digital regime with their architectural parable *Life: Supersurface*.[1] There are strange encounters within this project: free-roaming human families exposed to the even light of what can only be a virtual sun; bits and pieces of nature ordered into perfect squares; the forgotten debris of human-made objects scattered to invoke inhabitation. But it is the geometry of the grid, presented as the ultimate cosmological feature of humanity's earthly destiny and its transformation of nature that makes it an unforgettable project. Once seen it is very difficult to forget the photo-collages, their strange atmosphere and lighting, the clarity and immediacy of their shadows, the reflected clouds. These images have incredible staying power, as they weave together two traditionally opposing aesthetic, representational but also political realms: nature presented as the realism of texture, shade and depth, and culture presented as the ultimate abstraction, flatness, geometry and line. The project delivers a newly coherent image of total architecture, a utopian image so strong that it appears to balance on the verge of irony. This collage is not seamless, but the seams are conceptual as well as literal; they represent exact spots where the two realms meet, and in this way the grid becomes more an index and registration of this fateful meeting than a neutral background. It is no surprise that the project is presented under the umbrella title of 'Fundamental Acts' – there is indeed something fundamental at stake, something deeply convincing, potent with meaning and consequence, yet playful, poetic and light. To paraphrase Jeffrey Kipnis, *Life: Supersurface* might well be one of the 'Perfect Acts of Architecture'.[2]

THE GRID

Superstudio's grid is the precursor of the grid of the digital realm. This seems to be only a *superficial* observation at first glance, until we begin to understand the history both share. The first appearance of the grid as an ordering apparatus of modernity is usually attributed to Filippo Brunelleschi's invention and Leon Battista Alberti's formalisation of perspective in the 15th century. In their discovery of what was thought to be a systematic and scientific way to represent human vision, there was a seed of a much larger story – a first proposition of an autonomous and artificial apparatus that would in the time of a few centuries leave its human origin to become what we today call 'machine vision'. This was groundbreaking for many different reasons, but the most important was the underlying implication that vision is independent of light (and consequently, the divine *Lux* of the previous centuries), and fully dependent – as we would see in subsequent inventions of ever more complex but also less human vision apparatuses such as the radar – on geometry only. It is thus imperative to read the apparatus of perspective not for its verisimilitude to human vision, but to understand it precisely as a new kind of artificial vision that produces a new kind of space. The fact that there exists an apparatus of seeing that operates purely through geometry means that the contemporary designation of 'post-human' was deserved a long time ago.

THE SPACE OF MODERNITY

The second, even more profound implication of Brunelleschi's and Alberti's discovery was modern space itself. Before the invention of perspective, in the conceptual yet also quite literal sense, there was no space as we understand it

OPPOSITE
During their journey through
the game world, the player can
stumble upon places where the
grid ends abruptly, revealing the
violent meeting between nature
and geometry.

ABOVE
Superstudio's *Continuous Monument*
(1969), imagined as 'stage 2' of the
Supersurface computer game, is where
the game world transitions from realism
into pure geometric abstraction that will
eventually take off in flight.

THE FACT THAT
THERE EXISTS
AN APPARATUS
OF SEEING THAT
OPERATES PURELY
THROUGH GEOMETRY
MEANS THAT THE
CONTEMPORARY
DESIGNATION OF
'POST-HUMAN'
WAS DESERVED A
LONG TIME AGO

today. Medieval 'space' was a non-ordered, unsystematic overlapping of bodies in the divine medium, where the function that a body performed in the image had to do with its place in the cosmological narrative rather than its place in some 'real' space. The figures of important bodies were thus always bigger and more prominent than others, each modelled according to a series of rules conforming to the internal narrative the image was supposed to convey. Perspective changed that by introducing a new idea of universal space, a space that is even, measurable and equally potent in all directions, and whose ordering conforms to the fixed point of the observer's gaze. Now everything in the image conformed to this new ordering apparatus, and the most important index of this new space was the grid. Since then, the grid has quietly replaced the signs and registrations of previous cosmology to become the most prominent meta-model of modernity. The problem of architectural modelling from then on became a problem of relating the figure to the grid. The projects of Andrea Palladio, Claude-Nicolas Ledoux, Étienne-Louis Boulée, Le Corbusier, Mies van der Rohe and countless others can be clearly read as parts of this history.

This is the actual territory of Superstudio's project, and we can now appreciate just how profound their insight was. They transformed the grid from an index of modernity into the symbol of it, into an ultimate image that made radically visible something that was always lurking in the background, unchecked and unseen. They revealed the grid as the total ideological construct that held the Modernist project together, and proposed its final apotheosis in the form of total architecture, showing in the process that architecture was ever nothing but the grid, and that eventually it could be nothing more than it. Their insight is all the more powerful if we

TOP

The game world is filled with various objects for the player to discover and interact with. Repeating the formal idea of the scattered 'object plan', they also serve as keys and portals that open up new spaces.

ABOVE

Supersurface is designed as an environmental puzzle that can be arranged in various ways, where elements reveal and hide different aspects of its reality.

OPPOSITE

Spatial storytelling techniques set up conditions for the Superstudio parable to exist within the new medium.

take into account the advent of the digital in the late 20th century and its subsequent overtaking of the world. It is the very same vision technologies and the underlying spatial model ushered in during the Renaissance that are at work in the background of every digital project: digital objects are grids and every object is placed onto an ever-present ground grid. There is no escape from the grid.

THE SPACE OF THE DIGITAL

It is no surprise, then, that every visualisation of the space of the digital, from the 1982 film *Tron* and the imagining of early cyberspace, to the numerous user interfaces of the currently available 3D-modelling software, looks strangely similar to the Superstudio project. Generations of young people today, spending their time inside virtual worlds of computer games or creative software tools, actually live inside the Supersurface. The promise of a total utopia has been realised in software.

Making this condition explicitly visible was the main motivation behind the Supersurface computer game, developed in 2016 using the Unreal engine framework. The game belongs to the 'walking simulator' genre and uses its default first-person camera look. It employs environmental, indirect and nonverbal forms of storytelling in order to adapt the elusive, poetic parable of Superstudio to a new medium. There is no textual or verbal guidance – the player is free to roam endlessly in the landscape and interact with a variety of objects, scattered along the seams of two conflicting realities. The player soon discovers that the objects serve as portals that hold important information, as activating them opens up new ways of interacting with the game world and eventually allows entry into the large

floating primitives that reference another Superstudio project: *Continuous Monument* (1969).[3] The final act of the game directly references square number 50 of the storyboard for the *Continuous Monument* film, the caption for which reads: 'Then it begins to move and takes off in flight.'[4]

THE PROMISE OF
A TOTAL UTOPIA
HAS BEEN REALISED
IN SOFTWARE

Notes
1. Superstudio, *Life: Supersurface*, video (9:43), first shown as part of the 'Italy: The New Domestic Landscape' exhibition at the Museum of Modern Art (MoMA), New York, 26 May to 11 September 1972. The storyboards were published in *Casabella*, 367, 1972, pp 15–26.
2. Jeffrey Kipnis, *Perfect Acts of Architecture*, Museum of Modern Art (New York), 2001.
3. Superstudio, 'The Continuous Monument: An Architectural Model for Total Urbanisation', *Casabella*, 358, 1971.
4. *Ibid.*

Text © 2019 John Wiley & Sons Ltd. Images © Damjan Jovanovic

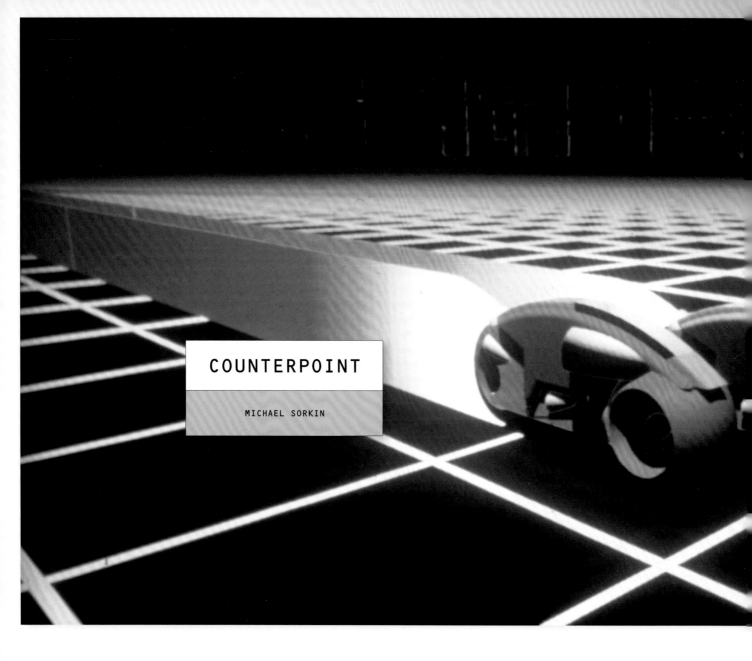

COUNTERPOINT

MICHAEL SORKIN

WHAT COMES AFTER THE AVANT-GARDE?

Still from *Tron*, 1982

Tron's light-cycle arena and sci-fi writer William Gibson's vision of 'cyberspace' were anticipated by Superstudio's *Continuous Monument* (1969) – all dystopic visions situated within relentless grids.

COUNTERPOINT
04/2019
№ 260

Architect, urbanist, writer and New York's *éminence grise* **Michael Sorkin** laments the lacuna of politic radical thought that he sees in the nostalgia for the 1960s and 1970s avant-garde, appropriated purely for its form-making, and warns that our historic navel-gazing will not solve anything.

'Avant-garde' is such a fossil. How is it relevant, except as fairly hip nostalgia, Photoshop sampler or pedigree by proxy and chops by association? The woolly bag of not-so-selective affinities rehearsed in this issue of Δ recalls a staple of Trump TV, that portrays as sour, comparisons by a cadre of 'presidential historians' (this seems to be an actual academic discipline) in which the exemplary qualities of some past prexy rebuke our current flamer-in-chief, held totally deficient in the integrity of Honest Abe or the command of command of FDR. These values do not actually matter to the Fake News discourse: fascination with the dear leader is total and his apparent control of the media seemingly complete; 24/7 of this a**hole befogs American culture, and whether the coverage is valanced left or right, we are all hypnotised.

I am not quite ready to argue that the Donald precisely occupies the position of an avant-garde artfully working to distinguish itself from the culture it seeks to bash and exceed, but if being 'avant' is measured in weirdness (there is no bypassing Mount Surrealism in this trek!), then maybe. Trump is just a few affective ticks (and tics) from whom – his co-generationalists Gilbert and George? Machine-tanned George Hamilton? Not really, but they are a succinct summa of key elements: personality, performance, peculiarity. The real art-Trumps are the likes of Jeff Koons, Damien Hirst and the 'ghost' of Jean-Michel Basquiat (ascended to the firmament of pure commodity), post-Andy swan dives into the murky waters of commerce and kitsch, the terrain of Trumpian branding, a lewd avant-garde, over the line but laughing all the way to the bank.

Can Anything Arty Ever Be Transgressive Again

But that is yesterday's spleen: marketised art annihilates the rest and nothing called art is dangerous for long. Insubordination and cock-snooting is another sure legacy of the Notorious A.G., but how to keep it up, how to actually sting? It is tough. The disarmament by globalisation of hip-hop (rapping in Mandarin or Urdu or Swedish) happened fast and furiously, gilding its initial critique with ornamental push-back: that 'gangsta' so upset parents, politicians and racists was as necessary to its ascent as the howls of the audience at the premiere of the *Rite of Spring*, 'public' outrage certifying their avant-juju cred. Who is outraged now? How transgressive can any formalism really be?

While membership of the avant-club is capacious (although surprisingly respectful of historical disciplinary categories), what is gathered in this Δ is all visual stuff: for us there is always a privileged relationship of sight and insight, and this retrospective sees almost entirely with its 'eyes'. This particular avant-garde is a branchless chain of filiation descending through a very specific, mainly European, clique of white guys, all self-identified as artists, skin still in the game: nobody just turns in their membership card and walks away. Their discordant, if

Demonstrators outside Trump Tower,
New York,
5 February 2019

In a world where public space is privatised and denuded, where politicians lie with fake news – why are architects not rallying against such notions, instead of conducting retrospective, formalist navel-gazing?

Bird's-eye View from South (Plan D-a: 720 Unit Scheme)

fundamentally harmless, acts of rupture try to overturn received practices by presenting themselves not simply as insubordinate, but as drastically *new*, and this pruned story is the default, rooted in Constructivism, Surrealism and their spawn, but without fessing up to any other affinitive origins (a Proun disrupts, an Impressionist merely paints) – as if ex novo. Practices and forms falling outside this skinny visual/ideological remit have no claims to the category.

What About the Others?

Art as critique is an inbred habit of modernity and a necessary, indeed central, component of the 'traditional' avant garde. But, in the official story told here, certain modes of reading are verboten, most prominently functionalism, taken for an operating manual rather than an aesthetic or a riposte. This is problematic for architecture, creating a constricted idea of utility and excluding big branches of a more expansive taxonomy. This issue does not, for example, want to touch an alternative avant-garde that includes Isambard Kingdom Brunel, the Bauhaus and Bucky. These are simply dumped in a materialist tip – teleologically inevitable, hence historical, hence historicised, hence irrelevant to breaking ranks. The preferred point of technological and formal origin for *our* avant-garde is Tatlin and Malevich and for ideological vibe (and, occasionally, a sense of humour), it is Man Ray or Marcel Duchamp, facilitating a quick leap to the post-Surrealism of the Situationists and to that over-reverenced caffe klatch of 'radical' Italians with their period rock-band brands, weirdly centre-stage in today's post-avant avant-garde.

But 'Super' or 'Zoom' never quite obscure the *guys* behind the curtain, claiming the conventional authority of originality and difference, but eventually selling out to the Man, their would-be world-warping polemics of resistance morphing into professorships

Michael Sorkin Studio,
Bonville Ecological Golf Resort, Coff's Harbour,
New South Wales,
Australia,
2014

Terreform operates in parallel with Michael Sorkin Studio, a 'commercial' design practice. The original idea was that the profits from the latter would subsidise the former. Terreform disrupts the status quo with its publishing and activities, working in a contemporary manner without reference to a retro avant-garde.

and the gridded laminate on designer coffee tables. One thing that is not avant about this bunch is their old-fashioned embrace of the figure of the protean artist super-hero who will change the world through beautiful acts of graphic terror. Paper tigers they may be, but they do encapsulate the core of how the avant-garde is vetted. First, by the clear immanence of subversively flavoured ideas (the world is all oppressive sameness, let us give people choices about how to live, geography is not destiny, we identify with the working class – it is all *in the picture*). Second by what is retrospectively clear as anticipation: in this case, Planet Digital (Superstudio predicts *Tron*). And finally, by that valiant disdain for the tectonics of actual inhabitation.

This favouring of the polemical over the aspirational (not that there is anything wrong with that) throws the weight of evaluation on the quality of desire rather than of effects. But the ideological vagueness – even slipperiness – makes it tough to locate either the frisson or the firmness of the connection. Why is Archigram's particular hyperbolic – or pastoral – overturning of spare, dead-end Modernism more avant-garde than Modernism's own overturning of its dark and stuffy predecessors? Because it is linguistically more up to date? Because it is so Woodstock-ishly sweet? Of course, desire must speak to be understood, but the format of comix (why

Given the Siamese
twinning of theory and
practice so urgent for
contemporary (or any)
avant-gardists, it is a
tad odd that nobody
seems to recall that this
discussion happened
decisively yonks ago

Terreform book covers

Radical design practice can take many forms,
including the support of comrades in struggle.
Terreform, a non-profit dedicated to urban
research and advocacy founded by Michael
Sorkin in 2005, provides a platform for
preoccupations that include the greening of
cities, the strengthening of social democracy,
ethical technologies and equitable policy
development.

is this the default?) does not tell us much except by too diffuse
association. Who does not do comix? Who cares about comix?
Who cares about another haunting artistic image of ubiquitous
alienation?

Strange Bedfellows and Partying On
I am disquieted by this trip down memory lane not because it hurts
to recall (or to party on), but because the operation is so *genetic*
– a 23 and Me origin tale of a retrospectively inevitable chain of
influences leading straight to our own deeply un-dangerous – if
delightful, even probing – operations. To be sure, there are some
charmingly odd cousins in the family and conversation at the
dinner table can get wonky as Pop and Digital and Logistical
operators duke it out: any avant-garde worth its salt must resist
pitching too big a tent and, while bedfellows can be strange, the
specific boundaries of any strangeness are dispositive. However,
when unabashed interpretation (hermeneutics and erotics *can*
fall in love) lapsed into Postmodern 'appropriation' – even
recuperating pastiche historicism as a cudgel – politics became a
joke. The resulting misalliance of André Breton and Robert Venturi
is at once false and canny, a reciprocally self-justifying brief
based not simply on their overturning ironies, but on their useful
celebration of a formalism thought to be simultaneously dangerous
and hermetic, on the violence of obscurity. The current generation
must gestate some serious and shocking freaks. Where are they?

Given the Siamese twinning of theory and practice so urgent for
contemporary (or any) avant-gardists, it is a tad odd that nobody
seems to recall that this discussion happened decisively yonks
ago – in the grand canon of Clement Greenberg, the Frankfurt
School and friends – usefully problematising the shifting role
of avant-garde practices in relation to 'high' and 'mass' culture

Gilets jaunes,
Paris,
9 February 2019

The Yellow Jackets stand in opposition to diminished buying power and increased fiscal burden, and are a social rebellion against the reduction of the French welfare state, mainly from the rural right.

Michael Sorkin Studio,
A New Capital City,
Xiongan,
China 2017

An avant-garde can be personal, the radical precursor of a long trajectory, the ontogeny that structurally mimics the phylogeny of broader currents. Sorkin's city designs show a private evolution from wild abstraction to more worldly precision.

and especially their dissipating dance with the co-optations of kitsch, and its tacky, infra-dig celebration of the forbidden. Our originary avant-gardes were underpinned by the radical theorisations of Marx and Freud. What is immanent today? There were those Chomskyan and Derridean blips (and now a wee flurry of interest in speculative realism whose anti-anthropocentrism does potentially align with some ecological theory – another story), but most of the actual (if conceptual) architects still need to be Sancho Panza-ed into their constructs by a critical-theoretical cohort representing newish forms of architectural aspirations to the metaphysical. This collapsing of reading and designing certainly bulks up the pretence, but remains a parallel substantiation rather than a deployable methodological insight, a neo-Surrealist cookbook. For that nowadays, we look to the richer, more insistent complications of the virtual, which have so radically altered the practicalities of practice while further embedding it – per Hardt and Negri *et al* – in a system we cannot stand outside of.

The digital Janus – whether via parametrics or just Photoshop – surely has the capacity to automate Surrealism and to yield weird and exquisite objects. But the exquisite never really threatens and the connoisseurship of rupture is a fool's errand. While the plurality of avant-gardes is vital, I would like to plump for a version that confronts real enemies – WalMart, CCTV, Facebook, climate change, inequality, racism, mass migration, neoliberalism, neocolonialism, Hollywood, homelessness, fascism. Can we have an architectural avant-garde as forceful and visually riveting as the *gilets jaunes* (who remind us that avant-gardist politics swing both ways)? As a rock through the window of Fauchon? As Gazan kids dancing a defiant dabke in the sniper kill zone that surrounds the Strip? ⌀

Text © 2019 Michael Sorkin. Images: pp 128–9 © pixeldreams.eu/Shutterstock; p 129(r) Photo Jeff Barnett-Winsby, courtesy of Michael Sorkin; p 130 © Erik McGregor/Pacific Press/LightRocket/Getty Images; pp 131, 133(b) © Michael Sorkin; p 132 Courtesy of Michael Sorkin; p 133(t) © Sameer Al-Doumy/NurPhoto/Getty Images

CONTRIBUTORS

Pablo Bronstein is an artist living and working in London and in Deal, Kent. Solo shows have included presentations at the Institute of Contemporary Arts (ICA), Royal Institute of British Architects (RIBA) and Bloomberg SPACE in London; at Nottingham Contemporary, Nottingham; Chatsworth House, Derbyshire; and the Metropolitan Museum of Art in New York. He was the recipient of the Tate Britain Commission 2016, for which he produced *Historical Dances in an Antique Setting* in the Duveen Galleries. He is the author of *Pseudo-Georgian London* (2017) and *Postmodern Architecture in London* (2011), published by König Books. Publications on the artist include Sam Jacob's *Pablo Bronstein: A is Building B is Architecture* (König Books, 2013).

Sarah Deyong is an associate professor and director of the architecture programme at the University of Nebraska-Lincoln, as well as an editorial board member of the *Journal of Architectural Education (JAE)* and the *Journal of the Society of Architectural Historians (JSAH)*. She received her PhD from Princeton University in New Jersey, and her BArch from the University of Toronto. With grants from the Graham Foundation and the Glasscock Center of the Humanities, her research has been published in the *Journal of Architecture, JAE, JSAH* and *Praxis*. Her essay 'Rethinking the Legacy of the Sixties' garnered the ACSA/JAE Best Scholarship of Design Award in 2015.

Sarah Dunn is a professor at the University of Illinois at Chicago, and co-director of architecture and urban design firm UrbanLab, based in the same city. She is the co-author of *UrbanLab: Bowling* (Applied Research + Design, 2017), which speculates on ways to realign architecture and infrastructure with dwindling natural resources. UrbanLab's work has been published and exhibited widely, including at the Venice Architecture Biennale (2010 and 2012) and the Chicago Architecture Biennial (2015 and 2017).

Martin Felsen is a Fellow of the American Institute of Architects (AIA), an associate professor at the Illinois Institute of Technology (IIT), and co-director of Chicago-based UrbanLab. In 2007 the practice won the History Channel's 'City of the Future' competition for Growing Water, a masterplan for Chicago, and in 2009 received the AIA College of Fellows Latrobe Prize.

Stylianos Giamarelos is an architect, historian and theorist of postmodern culture. He is a teaching fellow in architectural history, theory and interdisciplinary studies at the Bartlett School of Architecture, University College London (UCL), and an associate lecturer at the University of Greenwich. In 2008 he co-curated *ATHENS by SOUND*, the Greek national participation in the 11th Venice Architecture Biennale. He has been published in the *Journal of Architecture, JAE, Architectural Histories, Footprint, FRAME, San Rocco* and *Metalocus*. In 2018 he was a finalist runner-up for the biannual Publication Award of the European Architectural History Network.

Sam Jacob is principal of Sam Jacob Studio for architecture and design, a professor of architecture at the University of Illinois at Chicago, and a columnist for *Art Review* and *Dezeen*. He was previously a founding director of FAT Architecture. Recent projects include the V&A Gallery at Design Society, Shenzhen; 'Fear and Love' at the Design Museum, London; a new mixed-use building in London's Hoxton; and a landmark project with Mini Living for the London Design Festival. He has worked internationally on award-winning projects and has exhibited at major museums including the V&A, Museum of Applied Arts, Vienna, and the Art Institute of Chicago, as well as the Venice Architecture Biennale.

Damjan Jovanovic is an architect, educator and software designer based in Los Angeles. He is currently full-time faculty at the Southern California Institute of Architecture (SCI-Arc). He finished his postgraduate Master of Arts in Architecture degree at the Städelschule in Frankfurt in 2014, where he subsequently worked as a tutor and research associate. His work centres on the development of experimental architectural software, focusing on investigating the culture and aesthetics of software platforms, as well as questions of contemporary architectural education, authorship and creativity.

Andrew Kovacs is an assistant adjunct professor at the University of California, Los Angeles (UCLA) Architecture and Urban Design Department, where he teaches both undergraduate and graduate-level design studios. His design studio, Office Kovacs, works on projects at all scales from books, exhibitions and temporary installations to interiors, homes, speculative architectural proposals and public architecture competitions. His work has been published widely in the architectural press, including *A+U, Pidgin, Project, Pool, Perspecta, Manifest, Metropolis, Clog, Domus* and *The Real Review*. He is the creator and curator of Archive of Affinities, a widely viewed website devoted to the collection and display of architectural b-sides.

Perry Kulper is an architect and an associate professor at the University of Michigan in Ann Arbor. He previously taught at SCI-Arc for 17 years. After graduate studies at Columbia University in New York, he worked with Eisenman/Robertson, Robert AM Stern, and Venturi, Rauch and Scott Brown. His interests include the generative potential of drawing, the affordances of design methods, and broadening the conceptual range of architecture. He published *Pamphlet Architecture 34*, 'Fathoming the Unfathomable', with Nat Chard, in 2013. They are currently working together on a new book to be published by UCL Press.

Jimenez Lai is the founder of Los Angeles studio Bureau Spectacular. He currently teaches at UCLA and at Columbia University. His work is in the collections of the Museum of Modern Art (MoMA) in New York, San Francisco Museum of Modern Art (SFMOMA), Art Institute of Chicago and Los Angeles County Museum of Art (LACMA). His book, *Citizens of No Place*, was published by Princeton Architectural Press in 2012 with a grant from the Graham Foundation. In 2014 he represented Taiwan at the Venice Architecture Biennale. He previously lived in a desert shelter in Taliesin, and in a shipping container on the piers of Rotterdam.

Luis Miguel Lus Arana is an architect and researcher whose work deals with the exchanges between architecture and mass media (magazines, advertising, cinema and comics), and the history of visionary architecture and planning. He currently teaches Theory and History of Architecture at the University of Zaragoza, Spain. In his spare time he is also architectural cartoonist Klaus (Klaustoon).

Igor Marjanović is the JoAnne Stolaroff Cotsen Professor and Chair of undergraduate architecture programme at Washington University in St Louis. Trained both as an architect and architectural historian, he investigates the role of pedagogy, exhibitions and publications in the emergence of global architectural culture. His publications include *Drawing Ambience: Alvin Boyarsky and the Architectural Association* (Mildred Lane Kemper Art Museum and the RISD Museum of Art, 2014) and *Marina City: Bertrand Goldberg Urban Vision* (Princeton Architectural Press, 2010). He holds a PhD from the Bartlett School of Architecture, UCL, as well as degrees from the University of Illinois at Chicago and the University of Belgrade. He completed his diploma thesis at the Moscow Architectural Institute.

William Menking is co-founder and Editor-in-Chief of *The Architect's Newspaper* and a professor at Pratt Institute, New York. He was Commissioner of the US Pavilion 'Into the Open: Positioning Practice' at the 2008 Venice Architecture Biennale. He is the co-author of *Four Conversations on the Architecture of Discourse: Chicago, New York, London, Venice* (AA Publications, 2012), *Architecture on Display: On The History of the Venice Biennale of Architecture* (AA Publications, 2010), *Superstudio: Life Without Objects* (Skira, 2003) and *The Vienna Model: Housing for the 21st Century* (Jovis, 2016). He was 2011 Visiting Scholar at the University of California.

Michael Sorkin is President of Terreform, a non-profit dedicated to urban research and advocacy, and publisher of UR Books. He is Principal of Michael Sorkin Studio, an international design practice with a special focus on urbanism and 'green' architecture, and Distinguished Professor of Architecture and Director of the Graduate Program in Urban Design at the City College of New York. He has been architecture critic for *The Village Voice* and *The Nation*, contributing editor at *Architectural Record*, and author or editor of more than 20 books. He is a Fellow of the American Academy of Arts & Sciences, the recipient of the 2013 Cooper-Hewitt National 'Design Mind' Award, and a 2015 Guggenheim Fellow.

Neil Spiller is Editor of ⌂. He was previously Hawksmoor Chair of Architecture and Landscape and Deputy Pro Vice Chancellor at the University of Greenwich, London. Prior to this he was Vice Dean at the Bartlett School of Architecture, UCL. He has an international reputation as an architect, designer, artist, teacher, writer and polemicist. He is the founding Director of the Advanced Virtual and Technological Architecture Research Group (AVATAR), which continues to push the boundaries of architectural design and discourse in the face of the impact of 21st-century technologies. Its current preoccupations include augmented and mixed realities and other metamorphic technologies.

Neyran Turan is an architect and a partner at NEMESTUDIO, an architectural office that has been recognised with several awards, most recently the 2016 Architectural League New York Prize for Young Architects. She is currently an assistant professor at the Department of Architecture at the University of California, Berkeley. Her work focuses on alternative forms of environmental imagination and their capacity for new aesthetic and political trajectories within architecture and urbanism. She is founding chief-editor of the Harvard University Graduate School of Design (GSD) journal *New Geographies*. She has published in the *JAE, Perspecta, CARTHA, San Rocco, Conditions, MONU, Arqa* and *Thresholds*. In 2018 her book *Architecture as Measure* (Actar, 2019) was awarded a Graham Foundation grant.

Mimi Zeiger is a Los Angeles-based critic, editor and curator. Her work is situated at the intersection of architecture and media cultures. She has written for the *New York Times, Domus, Architectural Review* and *Architect*, of which she is a contributing editor. She is also an opinion columnist for *Dezeen*. She was one of the curators of the US Pavilion for the 2018 Venice Architecture Biennale. She also co-curated 'Now, There: Scenes from the Post-Geographic City', which received the Bronze Dragon award at the 2015 Bi-City Biennale of Urbanism\Architecture in Shenzhen. She teaches in the Media Design Practices MFA programme at the ArtCenter College of Design in Pasadena, California, and is a visiting professor at SCI-Arc.

What is *Architectural Design*?

Founded in 1930, *Architectural Design* (△) is an influential and prestigious publication. It combines the currency and topicality of a newsstand journal with the rigour and production qualities of a book. With an almost unrivalled reputation worldwide, it is consistently at the forefront of cultural thought and design.

Each title of △ is edited by an invited Guest-Editor, who is an international expert in the field. Renowned for being at the leading edge of design and new technologies, △ also covers themes as diverse as architectural history, the environment, interior design, landscape architecture and urban design.

Provocative and pioneering, △ inspires theoretical, creative and technological advances. It questions the outcome of technical innovations as well as the far-reaching social, cultural and environmental challenges that present themselves today.

For further information on △, subscriptions and purchasing single issues see:

http://onlinelibrary.wiley.com/journal/10.1002/%28ISSN%291554-2769

Volume 88 No 4
ISBN 978 1119 337843

Volume 88 No 5
ISBN 978 1119 328148

Volume 88 No 6
ISBN 978 1119 375951

Volume 89 No 1
ISBN 978 1119 453017

Volume 89 No 2
ISBN 978 1119 500346

Volume 89 No 3
ISBN 978 1119 546023

Individual backlist issues of △ are available as books for purchase starting at £29.99 / US$45.00

www.wiley.com

How to Subscribe
With 6 issues a year, you can subscribe to △ (either print, online or through the △ App for iPad)

Institutional subscription
£310 / $580
print or online

Institutional subscription
£388 / $725
combined print and online

Personal-rate subscription
£136 / $215
print and iPad access

Student-rate subscription
£90 / $137
print only

△ App for iPad
6-issue subscription:
£44.99 / US$64.99
Individual issue:
£9.99 / US$13.99

To subscribe to print or online
E: cs-journals@wiley.com

Americas
E: cs-journals@wiley.com
T: +1 781 388 8598
or +1 800 835 6770
(toll free in the USA & Canada)

Europe, Middle East and Africa
E: cs-journals@wiley.com
T: +44 (0) 1865 778315

Asia Pacific
E: cs-journals@wiley.com
T: +65 6511 8000

Japan (for Japanese-speaking support)
E: cs-japan@wiley.com
T: +65 6511 8010
or 005 316 50 480
(toll-free)

Visit our Online Customer Help available in 7 languages at www.wileycustomerhelp.com/ask

NOW available on the iPad!

- Buy single issues or subscribe
- Store all downloaded issues to your personal library
- Easily navigable format brings new life to △ articles
- Free to personal print subscribers

Available on the App Store